Ingolf Cruiser

The Danish Ingolf-Expedition

Ingolf Cruiser

The Danish Ingolf-Expedition

ISBN/EAN: 9783337723750

Printed in Europe, USA, Canada, Australia, Japan

Cover: Foto ©ninafisch / pixelio.de

More available books at **www.hansebooks.com**

THE DANISH

INGOLF-EXPEDITION.

VOL. II, PART I.

CONTENTS:

PUBLISHED AT THE COST OF THE GOVERNMENT

BY

THE DIRECTION OF THE ZOOLOGICAL MUSEUM OF THE UNIVERSITY.

COPENHAGEN.

H. HAGERUP.

BIANCO LUNO (F. DREYER), PRINTER TO THE COURT.

1899.

THE DANISH INGOLF EXPEDITION.

VOLUME II.

1.

THE ICHTHYOLOGICAL RESULTS.

BY

CHR. LÜTKEN.

-

WITH 4 PLATES, 1 MAP, 2 FIGURES IN THE TEXT AND A LIST OF THE STATIONS.

COPENHAGEN.

BIANCO LUNO (F. DREYER), PRINTER TO THE COURT.

1898.

The Ichthyological Results of the Expeditions of the „Ingolf".

By Chr. Lütken.

THE oceanic ichthyological earnings of the 2 expeditions of the Ingolf in 1895 and 1896 are in so far rather considerable as they comprise c. 29 genera and c. 44 species; but they do not comprise many types which are new, viz. not known or described in our own days or in earlier times. But they number several forms which were not formerly known at our museum or from the northern seas more accessible to us, and there are species among them which have been known hitherto in few specimens only and thus from a very limited study-material. The knowledge of the distribution of several types is therefore now extended, as also the knowledge of their occurrence over an area hitherto little examined, and an addition somewhat considerable is thence procured to the earnings of the earlier expeditions of the Challenger, le Talisman, le Travailleur, the Blake, the Albatross, the Vöringen, the Knight Errant, l'Hirondelle and the Princesse Alice etc.

It was so far a disappointment that the expedition did not forward us several rather well known arctic or abyssal types that might have been expected, f. i. apodal *Lophioidei*, arctic picked dog-fishes, *Aphanopus* etc. The impossibility of using the weel of the prince of Monaco in seas of a northern and troublesome character and the difficulties, to say the least, of using angles must wear the blame for the deficiencies in this respect. The types, which will be specially mentioned in the following sheets and partly figured in the accompanying plates, are chiefly *Cottoidei* (in the wider, older sense of the word), the *Lycodes*, *Liparides* and allied types (*Paraliparis*), *Rhodichthys*, *Macrurus* and other deep-sea *Gadoids* and deep-sea fishes (*Hepocephalus*, *Antimora*), deep-sea-*Murænoids*, *Notacanthini* and certain *Raja*-species. That the account of *Scopelini* is rather scarce is due to the difficulties of capturing those fragile fishes. That the results as here exposed may be found somewhat uncertain in several cases in certain difficult genera – owing in part to my personal defects, I shall not deny, but I hope that the special difficulties of those cases will be my excuse. The number of the plates I have reduced to the most necessary. I have specially made use of the colored sketches made on board of the Ingolf of animals still living or freshly caught, which made it possible to produce some colored figures.

Mr. Adolph Jensen has been kind enough to assist me with the revision of the manuscript and in other ways; I owe to him several important corrections and emendations and bestow on him my best thanks for his aid.

Skates (Rays): the genus *Raja*.

Raja hyperborea Collett.

Collett: Den norske Nordhavs Expedition. Fiskene. p. 9, pl. I, fig. 1 2.

Günther: Report on the deep-sea fishes. Expedition of the Challenger. p. 8, pl. IV, A, B, C.

Also figured in Goode & Bean: Oceanic Ichthyology , pl. IX, fig. 28, and by Smitt in Skandinaviens Fiskar , p. 1110 11, fig. 317 18.

The Norvegian North-sea-expedition caught a male specimen, about 20 inches (518^{mm}) long at a depth of 459 fathoms, 115 kilometres West of Spitzbergen (Norskoerne). The Knight Errant captured in the Faroe-Channel a larger male, 24^1 $_2$ inches long, at 608 fathoms together with 2 smaller females (6^1 , inches) and a female (8 inches); a very young male was captured at 400 fathoms. On the Ingolf -expeditions were caught 3 specimens, 2 females and a male, similar in size to those of the Voringen . The localities were the following:

Station 113 (to the south of Jan Mayen), 69° 31′ Lat. North, 7 06′ Longitud. West, the depth 1309 fathoms. Temperature at the bottom ÷ 1 .0 C., nature of the bottom: *Biloculina*-clay. A female, 24³/₄ inches long from the point of the snout to the end of the tail, greatest breadth 20¹/₂ inch.

Station 140 (North of the Faroe Islands), 63° 29′ Lat. North, 6 57′ Long. West, depth 780 fathoms. Temperature at the bottom + 0. 9 C., its nature: gray mud. A female, its length 21¹ , inch, breadth 17 inches.

Station 141 (North of the Faroe Islands), 63 22′ Lat. North, 6″ 58′ Long. West, depth 679 fathoms. Temperature at the bottom +0².6 C. Gray mud. Male: length 25 inches, breadth 18 inches.

The description of Prof. Collett may be compared with that of Dr. Günther, *loco citato*. In this Arctic Ray there is apparently no difference according to age in the physiognomy, contour etc. Nevertheless it should be noted, that the delicate dorsal spinous clothing has a larger or more complete extension in the young specimen figured by Günther than in the known larger individuals. The differences attributable to individual variation and appearing by a comparison between the specimens of Collett and Günther are enumerated by Lilljeborg (Sveriges och Norges Fiskar III, p. 604) and by Smitt (Skandinaviens Fiskar p. 1112).

I shall add some remarks on the variations in shape, spinnlation etc. which make themselves apparent when comparing the specimens before me, two of which are females. The typical specimen of Collett has on both sides 3 larger spines in a series inside of the upper margin of the eye, the first pair before a line between the anterior margin of the eyes, the hindmost close behind a line between the posterior margin of the parietal foramina. There are further 2 pair of shoulder spines and in the middle line of the body a series of 26 spines and a small spine between the 2 dorsal fins. This little spine is wanting in all our 3 specimens and should therefore be omitted in the specific diagnosis. The supraorbital spines are in all as indicated above, if one of them is not lost on one side, as is apparently the case in one of them. The shoulder spines may be in 2 or 3 pairs. In the unpaired dorsal line the number of spines may be from 21 to 31. The teeth are delicate and acute and show no sexual difference with the exception that one female (from station 140) is almost quite toothless. Two of our specimens are on the back uniformly dark brown, as are those from the

-Voringen -expedition; the third, a male, is adorned with numerous light specks which are however not sharply defined. On the belly this specimen is generally dark with some rather regularly distributed smaller or larger light spots; the surroundings of the mouth are white. The other female is light on the lower side of the head and on the whole median party near to the anus, but else dark. The male is generally light on the ventral side with darker patches in a fashion similar to the specimen of the Voringen , but with greater preponderance of the white or colorless parts. In the female with the dark belly the first dorsal fin is proportionally very small. The cards are relatively little developed on the back of the pectoral fins of our male, and its *appendices genitales* are not larger than in the Norvegian typical specimen (ab. 2 inches); therefore all the specimens hitherto obtained of this sex and species are relatively young, though of a rather considerable size. The flat lower surface of the tail is continued as a low dermal fold at both sides.

Raja ingolfiana Ltk. n. sp. (Tab. 1, fig. 1.).

Thus I name provisionally a male specimen of *Raja* -- very young, judging from its little developed *appendices genitales* (scarcely an inch long), captured by the Ingolf -expedition at Station 32 (off Holstensborg) at a depth of 318 fathoms on 66 35′ Lat. North, 56 38′ Long. West, where the bottom was brownish-gray mud with very numerous *Rhabdammina* and some pebbles, the bottom temperature of the water 3.9° C. This probably new species belongs to the less acutely pointed species; measured in the usual manner the length of the snout equals half the breadth over the middle line of the eyes. The external angles of the disk are more rounded, less acutely pointed, its anterior margins more straight, less sinuous than in *R. hyperborea*, the external laps of the ventral fins less narrow. The tail is much stouter, both longer and more robust; its length is 12 inches, the distance from the point of the snout to the origin of the tail 13$^1/_2$ inches, the total lenght thus 25$^1/_2$ inch. 2 4 supraorbital spines may be counted, some smaller ones on the back of the snout, and some scapular spines (3 placed in a triangle); in the median line of the tail and the back a dense series of 47 spines and along the lateral margins of the tail (where the lateral folds are in *R. hyperborea*) a dense series of somewhat smaller spines. There are no spines between the dorsal fins which are placed close together. Otherwise the dorsal face is only slightly spinulous with few isolated spinules and the ventral face is quite naked. Between the medial series of spines on the tail and the 2 lateral series is on both sides a zone of numerous, hardly visible asperities (spinelets); the dorsal fins are clothed in the same manner, but the ventral ones naked. The teeth are small and pointed. The ventral face of the body is whitish without spots, only with some dark parts on the lower face of the tail and the ventral fins, and delicately furrowed; the dorsal surface is brown.

Before this species can be studied in both sexes and different ages its place in the series of types in the family of Rays can not be fixed. Of the many Eastamerican species only *R. crinaceus* and *ocellata* have been accessible to me, none of the more pointed species. I shall refer the reader to S. W. Garmans memoir On the Skates (*Raja*) of the eastern coast of the United States in the Proceedings of the Boston Society of Natural History , Vol. XVII (1874), p. 170 etc., to Goode and Beans Oceanic Ichthyology (1895) p. 24 30, to Gilberts The ichthyological collections of the

1'

U. S. fish commission steamer Albatross (Report U. S. Comm. Fish etc.) 1896 and to Jordan and Evermanns: The fishes of North and Middle America (Bulletin United States National Museum Nr. 47, 1896), p. 67—76.

Raja rostro acutiusculo, pinnis pectoralibus antice rotundatis, cauda sat robusta, spinis nonnullis supraorbitalibus, rostralibus et scapularibus, c. 47 in parte mediana dorsi et caudæ, interpinnalibus caudæ nullis.

Raja Fyllæ Ltk. (Tab. II, fig. 2).

R. ornata Garman?

A male specimen captured on Station **25** off Godthaab (63°30' Lat. North, 54°25' Long. West, at 582 fathoms, at a temperature at the bottom of 3°.3 C.), which has a length of 555^{mm} (about 21 inches) and a greatest diameter of the disk of 310^{mm} (11³/₄ inches), and whose large *appendices genitales* demonstrate that it is adult and capable of procreation, agrees else completely with another specimen somewhat smaller (470^{mm}), taken in 1889 in the Denmark Strait at 426 fathoms, and referred by me (Videnskabelige Meddelelser fra den naturhistoriske Forening 1891, p. 32) to the *Raja Fyllæ*, established not long time before (ibid. 1887, p. 1—4, pl. I) by me as a new species on a younger female specimen from the same seas. This specimen, which is thus the proper original specimen of the species, had, to be sure, in many respects another aspect, and it was therefore with some doubt that I identified the adult male from the Denmark Strait (1889) with the young female from the Davis Strait (1884). I was induced to this determination by the fact, that other species of Rays were not known at that time from the Greenland seas than *Raja Fyllæ* and *R. radiata*, and by the examination of a couple of still younger males from the Davis Strait (likewise from 1889). The new capture from 1895 induced me to take up the question again and to examine as far as possible, if the difference of age or sex is so large as supposed by me or if a specific difference had been overlooked. The two elder specimens I shall mention together, designating however the larger figured Ingolfian specimen (from 1895) as No. I, the somewhat smaller one (from 1889) as No. II.

The incisions of the margins of the disk (at the height of the parietal foramina) are still sharper defined in No. I than in No. II. The other portion of the pectoral fin is rounded in a corresponding manner in both. The genital appendages are 110^{mm} long in No. I, 105^{mm} in No. II. There are larger and smaller spines in a marginal zone more or less broad, commencing at the point of the snout and terminating somewhat before the terminal portion of the groups of pectoral cards- which are generally speaking comprised in the said zone; the following zone, comprising the rest of the back of the pectoral fins and of the trunk, is naked with the exception of the proper median party, which begins at the point of the snout, embraces the interorbital space and is continued over the median portion of the trunk and the whole backside of the tail. Covered with larger spines of the *R. radiata*-type are especially the back of the snout, the space between the eyes especially the supraorbital margin, a rather broad scapular party with many spines and a broad zone at the median part of the back, continued on and covering the whole dorsal part of the tail. According to the more or less pronounced stoutness of the tail, there may be counted 3, 4 or 5 spines beside each other, forming rather regular rows, with numerous fine or somewhat larger spinules on the lateral margins of this part of the body. The teeth are small, fine and pointed; I counted c. 34 rows from one corner of the mouth to the other. The dorsal fins are closely approximated, not even completely separated. The specimen No. I is light grayish on the back, uniformly dark on the belly; on the other hand No. II is quite white on the belly, light brownish-grayish on the back. On the ventral face there are, as most commonly in the Skates, no thorns at all.

A younger male, 201^{mm} long and 106^{mm} broad, from the Davis Strait (235 fathoms) with minute genital appendices is mentioned by me previously (l. c. 1891, p. 32). I therefore restrain myself to some brief remarks on this specimen, compared with the here described adult males. The point of the snout is hardly visible as such. The pectoral margin of the disk is slightly sinuous, not forming a quite straight line; but a sharp incision does not occur. The back is quite covered with small spines until towards the posterior margin of the pectoral fins; also the ventral fins are partially thorny, while at a later stage they are naked. But between this uniform clothing of the trunk, the fins and the tail some spines a little larger make their appearance, some on the back of the snout. 3 pairs of supra-orbitals, one pair of suprascapulars and a single row of about 37 in the median line of the back, commencing behind the head and continued almost to the dorsal fins on the tail   accompanied on the back of the tail by middle-sized spines forming the transition to the general clothing with spinelets. Thus during the growth of the animal a rich development of larger spines takes place untill the above described stage of evolution is attained. The

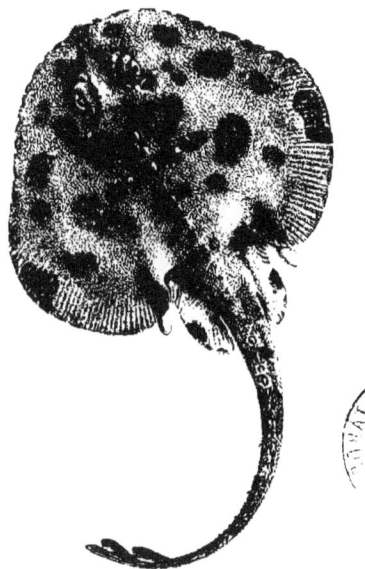

Raja Fyllæ jun. fem. The typical specimen, somewhat diminished.

color of the back is brown with some more or less distinct round specks and 2 lighter parties on each pectoral, rather posteriorly. The ventral surface is light with brownish spots and marbled.

A still younger male, 115^{mm} long and 60^{mm} broad, likewise from the Davis Strait at 289 fathoms depth, has no distinct point of the snout and no sinuation of the margin of the disk. The spinulation is essentially the same as in the first described younger male, with the difference that there are a few more supraorbital and scapular spines (a group of three on each side of the median line) and that on the tail only the median series is of a superior size. The dorsal surface is handsomely painted with larger or smaller round spots or belts (on the tail) which partially also are apparent on the thinner portion of the pectorals and ventrals.

The young female, previously described and figured by me   historically then the type of the species   198ᵐᵐ in length and 101ᵐᵐ in breadth - from the Davis Strait at the depth of 80 fathoms, resembles the younger males just bespoken, especially the youngest, in shape, spinulation and coloring, which it is not necessary to specify nearer, as the actual reproduction here in the text (p. 5) gives the necessary details. It may be observed however that the colored spots are much smaller than in the smallest male at hand. As older females are not at hand, it can not yet be said if those will habitually be more like the adult male, or how great the difference will turn out between the sexes in the sexually mature state.

Raja ornata Garman which has only been better known to me from fig. 24 of the Oceanic Ichthyology resembles so much to my *R. Fyllæ*, that it would desire a closer examination to determine if it is not the same species, what perhaps is not unlikely. It must be observed however that of the specimens hitherto bespoken of *R. ornata* the typical specimen is from Florida (Alligator Key) at 138 fathoms, the 3 others from 142 fathoms at 32 24′ Lat. North, 78 44′ Long. W., thus from a much more southern zone, a circumstance that might weaken the presumption of this identity, for whose confirmation an immediate comparison would be necessary.

Deep-sea-Eels: *Synaphobranchus* and *Nemichthys (Serrivomer)*.

Of the former genus of deep-sea-eels the Ingolf has brought home 2 specimens, that I have been able to compare with a specimen of *Synaphobranchus pinnatus* from the Northamerican deep-sea expeditions.

Under the name of *Synaphobranchus pinnatus* is mentioned in the Catalogue of fish collected and described of L. Th. Gronov edited by J. E. Gray (1854), a Murænoid described in the Museum Ichthyologicum of Gronov, II, p. 11, Nr. 161, which typical specimen was however wanting in Gronovs collection and therefore not passed to the British Museum, when the museum purchased the said collection. But Johnson & Lowe obtained some specimens at Madeira and the latter described it as *Synaphobranchus Kaupii* (Proceed. Zool. Soc. 1862, p. 169). After Dr. Günther having in his Catalogue of Fishes in the British Museum (VIII, 1874) renamed it with the specific name of Gray and Gronov, it occurs now in the ichthyological literature again as *Synaphobranchus pinnatus*. The American deep-sea-investigations have demonstrated its occurrence at depths of 304- 740 fathoms in the sea off the eastern shores of the United States (f. inst. between the St. George bank and South-Carolina). Goode og Bean in Bull. Mus. Comp. Zool. X, p. 223 enumerate 84 specimens from 33° 39 Lat. North and 65 -76 Long. West. Compare the Oceanic Ichthyology p. 143, fig. 164. A great number of Stations is enumerated. The expedition of the Challenger discovered it in greater or smaller numbers of specimens at different stations (off Brasil, south of Japan and south of the Philipines etc.) at depths of 214 1200 fathoms. The French expeditions (le Travailleur , le Talisman) have brought together a great number (56) of specimens from the coast of Marocco and the west coast of North

Africa, from the Azores and from the Canarian and Capoverdian islands and from depths between 405 og 3200 Metres. Also the prince of Monaco obtained it at the Azores in great numbers, in several draughts of the weel, partly in the company of *Simenchelys parasiticus*, relatively 251 and 328 specimens. Compare: Collett's Résultats des campagnes scientifiques, Poissons p. 154. The *S. pinnatus* is figured by Günther (Report on deep-sea fishes pl. 62, fig. A) and by Vaillant (Expéditions scientifiques p. 88, pl. 6, fig. 2). Other species of the same genus are figured and described: *S. bathybius* Gthr. (south of Japan, in the northern part of the Pacific and between Cape and Kerguelen, Report on deep-sea fishes p. 254, pl. 62, fig. B), at 1375–2050 fathoms, perhaps identical with *Histiobranchus infernalis* Gill. (Proc. Un. St. Nat. Mus. VI, 1884. p. 255), The Atlantic: 38° 30' 30" Lat. North, 69° 08' 25" Long. West, depth 1731 fathoms. Compare also the Oceanic Ichthyology p. 145, fig. 165. The authors of this work take the genera *Synaphobranchus* and *Histiobranchus* as different, partly also the species of *H. bathybius* and *H. infernalis*, and it would therefore be the most correct thing to retain the later name for the northatlantic type. Further: *S. brevidorsalis* Gthr. (l. c. p. 255, pl. 63, fig. C) from North of New Guinea and South of Japan (345–1070 fathoms).

Ingolf captured 2 specimens of a *Synaphobranchus* (or, according to Goode and Bean, of a *Histiobranchus*), 16 and 18½ inch. long, at the stations 36 and 37 on 61° 50' Lat. North, 56° 21' Long. West and on 60° 17' Lat. North, 54° 05' Long. W., depth 1435 and 1715 fathoms where the bottom was a grayish or light chocolate-coloured mud and the bottom-temperature 1.5 or 1°.4 C. It will be sufficient to state of those *Histiobranchi* of the Ingolf, that the small pectorals (of the length of the snout) the position of the anus and the fact that the dorsal fin reaches almost to the head, make it evident that they do not belong to *Synaphobranchus pinnatus*, but either to *H. bathybius* or to Gill's *H. infernalis*, if these are not synonyms.

The geografical distribution of the same species will at the same time be elucidated as far as it is known at present.

Nemichthys (Serrivomer) Beanii Gill & Ryder.

Of this species Ingolf captured on the Stations 12 and 20, at 64° 38' Lat. North, 32° 37' Long. West, and on 58° 20' Lat. North, 40° 48' Long. W., in the Denmark Strait and S. S. E. of Cape Farewell, at a depth of 1040 and 1695 fathoms, on a bottom of soft mud with pebbles and a bottom-temperature of 0°.3 and 1°.5 C. two not fully well preserved specimens of the said deep-sea-eel-genus. A third somewhat better was obtained at Station 45: 61° 32' Lat. N. and 9° 43' Long. W., West of the Faroe Islands on a depth of 643 fathoms, light gray muddy bottom with *Globigerina*-shells and a bottom-temperature of 4°.17 C. It is a rather large specimen, 26 inches long; it is noted in the zoological Journal of the expedition in the following manner: lower side of the head quite black, the sides of the trunk and back bronzeously gilt with numerous fine black points».

Goode and Bean have in the »Oceanic Ichthyology» given a figure (fig. 175) of *Serrivomer Beanii* Gill & Ryder which agrees well with the 3 specimens at hand. The shape is much elongated, the length of the head from the point of the beak to the branchial fissure being contained 6 7 times in the total length, further on somewhat compressed and tapering to a long pointed tail, whose length reckoned from the anus is three fourths of the total length. The jaws are moderately elongated, the length of the upper jaw measured from the anterior margin of the eye is contained twice and a half in the whole length of the head. The mouth reaches backwards under the eyes, which are not absolutely small. The branchial openings are very wide, obliquely placed slits in the median ventral line, almost continuous. The jaws are armed with fine teeth, and the vomer wears a long series of densely placed pointed teeth. The very small pectorals are placed at the upper end of the branchial slit. The dorsal fin is represented by a series of very delicate and short rays beginning somewhat behind the anus, also the rays of the anal fin are very feeble, but perhaps somewhat longer. The soft blue-black skin is more or less lacerated in all the 3 specimens but partially preserved. The measures are the following:

Total length	680^{mm}	570^{mm}	510^{mm}
The length of the head to the branchial slit	100 -	93 -	85 -
The length of the beak to the corners of the mouth . . .	42 -	37 -	35 -
Trunk and head from the point of the snout to the anus	170 -	135 -	123 -
Length of the tail from the anus	510 -	435 -	387 -

The *Serrivomer Beanii* was known hitherto from a single specimen caught by the Albatross at 41° 40′ 30″ Lat. North, 65° 28′ 30″ Long. W. and at 855 fathoms depth. It is described by Gill and Ryder in 1883 (Proc. U. S. Nat. Mus. VI, p. 260) together with a related type *Spinivomer Goodei*, also taken by the Albatross in the northern Atlantic likewise in a single specimen. Both the generic names are derived from the armature of the vomer with large teeth. Goode and Bean have in the Oceanic Ichthyology p. 155 distinguished them as a separate group of nemichthyid muraenoids: *Spinivomeridae*, to which is further referred the *Nemichthys (Serripes) Richardi* Vaill., captured by the Talisman at the Azores on 2995 fathoms and originally considered by Vaillant (Exp. scientifiques Travailleur et Talisman , p. 93, pl. VII, fig. 1 1 a) as identic with Günthers: *Nemichthys infans* (Chall. Rep. vol. XXII, p. 264, pl. 63), but in the Appendice (p. 385) to the said work established as a separate species.

Alepocephalus Agassizii Goode et Bean.

Besides the *A. rostratus* already known to Risso from the Mediterranean and from adjoining parts of the Atlantic as far as the Azores, the Canarian and Capoverdian islands for which species besides the older figures by Risso and Valenciennes I may refer to Vaillants Expéditions scientifiques (pl. XI and XII) and to Oceanic Ichthyology (p. 36, fig. 41) some other atlantic species have been described especially by American ichthyologists: *A. Agassizii* G. B., *A. productus* Gill, *A. Bairdii* G. B., *Conocara Mc. Donaldi* G. B. and *A. (C.) macropterus* Vaill., for which species I may refer to Oceanic Ichthyology p. 37 39, fig. 45, 46, 47, 48 og 43. A further addition is *A. Giardi* (Koehler: Résultats scientifiques de la campagne du Caudan , Annales de l'Université de Lyon fasc. III, p. 513, pl. XXVI, fig. 1) at a depth of 800 1410 metres, Bay of Biscay. On the second cruise of the Ingolf was obtained an *Alepocephalus*, 20^1/$_4$ inch long (530^{mm}), no doubt an *A. Agassizii*, at

Station 83: 62° 25′ Lat. N., 28′ 30′ Long. W., at a depth of 912 fathoms, S. W. of Iceland, with a bottom-temperature of 3°.5 C. The height of the body is contained somewhat more than 5 times (1 : 5.3) in the total length, reckoned to a line between the points of the caudal fin; the length of the head (164ᵐᵐ) is one third of the total length (to the cleft of the caudal fin); the diameter of the eye equals the distance from the eye to the point of the snout, not one fourth of the length of the head; the upper jaw terminates in a line with the posterior border of the pupil; the breadth of the somewhat hollow front is somewhat smaller than the ocular diameter or the snout.

On the southern and eastern hemisphere *Alepocephalus* is partly represented by *Bathytroctes*, which should perhaps be united with *Alepocephalus*. Of the 10 species enumerated in ‹Oceanic Ichthyology› 7 are Atlantic.

Scopelini.

Species of *Scopelus* are caught at 8 ‹stations›, but they have almost all suffered so much from their being taken in dredges or the trawls, that the light-spots are only visible in part. Some specimens I have identified as *S. elongatus*; the others belong to the less elongate species. The following list therefore tells, that in the zone traversed by the ‹Ingolf› between 61° and 65° Lat. North are to be found the species of *Scopelus* enumerated at the noted depths, on the bottom, if they are not captured during the hawling up of the implements used; but experience will also show that it is not through bottom fishery, that one may procure a good material of these animals, equalling that furnished by the surface.

I refer the reader to my ‹Bidrag til nordisk Ichthyographi VIII. Nogle nordiske Laxesild (Scopelini) in the ‹Videnskabelige Meddelelser fra den naturhistoriske Forening i Kjobenhavn , 1881, and to ‹Spolia Atlantica, Scopelini Musei Zoologici etc.› (K. D. Vid. Selsk. Skrifter 6. Række, VII, 6).

Stat.	Lat. N.	Lgtd. W.	Fathoms		
12:	64° 38′	32° 37′	1040	(Denmark Strait, W. of Iceland) *Sc. elongatus* Risso and *Sc. glacialis* Rhdt.	
17:	62° 49′	26° 55′	745	(S. W. of Iceland) *Scop. arcticus* Ltk.	
25:	63° 30′	54° 25′	582	(W. of Godthaab) *Scop. arcticus* Ltk.	
27:	64° 54′	55° 10′	393	(S. W. of Sukkertoppen) *Scop. glacialis* Rhdt.	
35:	65° 16′	55° 05′	362	(same place) *Scop. glacialis* Rhdt.	
40:	62° 00′	21° 36′	845	(S. of Iceland) *Scop. elongatus* Risso.	
81:	61′ 44′	27° 00′	485	(S. W. of Iceland)	*Scop. glacialis* Rhdt.
141:	63° 22′	6° 58′	679	(East of Iceland)	

Cyclothone (Gonostoma) microdon Gthr.

For this widely diffused species I shall refer to my remarks in my «Korte Bidrag til nordisk Ichthyographi VIII (‹Videnskabelige Meddelelser fra den naturhistoriske Forening› 1891, p. 216—19, article 5 on *Gonostoma (Cyclothone) microdon* Gthr. and to my description and figure in my ‹Spolia Atlantica, Scopelini Musei Zoologici etc.» (K. D. Vid. Selsk. Skr. (6) VII, 6, tab. II, fig. 4—5). At an early time (1843) we got this little Scopelid from the Baffin Bay. The «Challenger Expedition› got it from many places in the Atlantic (both in its northern and southern parts) and in the indo-pacific sea (S. of Japan, N. of New Guinea, off Amboina etc.). Other localities are cited by Vaillant (l. c., *Neostoma quadrioculatum*), by Alcock (Ann. Mag. Nat. Hist. 1889, p. 399, the Bengal Bay and the Andamans at 265—485 fathoms), by Collett (Campagnes scientifiques , p. 130), and by Gilbert (The ichthyol. Coll. of the U. S. F. C. St. Albatross», Report U. S. Comm. Fish. a. Fisheries for 1893, p. 402, the Bering-Sea) and in Oceanic Ichthyology p. 100. The distribution of the species turns out to be almost cosmopolitic. The latter work cites besides the *C. microdon (lusca* G. & R.) *C. bathyphila* Vaill., *C. elongata* Gthr. (*stigmaticus* Gill.), *C. gracilis* Gthr. and *C. quadrioculatus* Vaill., already mentioned as probably identical with *C. microdon*. On the expeditions of the Ingolf» the *C. microdon* has several times been captured as appears in rather deep water; some of the specimens are, it is true, rather damaged. The station-list given below will at least illustrate the frequency of these small fishes in the subarctic zone of which it treats.

Station	Lat. N.	Lgtd. W.	Fath.	
9:	64° 18'	27° 00'	295	West of Iceland.
11:	64° 34'	31° 12'	1300	West of Iceland.
12:	64 38'	32° 37'	1040	West of Iceland (numerous specimens).
17:	62 49'	26° 55'	745	Southwest of Iceland.
18:	61° 44'	30° 29'	1135	Entrance of Denmark Strait.
21:	58 01'	44° 45'	1330	South of Greenland.
25:	63° 30'	54° 25'	582	Southwest of Godthaab.
36:	61 50'	56° 21'	1435	Southwest of Sukkertoppen.
40:	62 00'	21 36'	845	South of Iceland.
67:	61° 30'	22° 30,	975	Southwest of Iceland.
76:	60 50'	26° 50'	806	Southwest of Iceland.
81:	61 44'	27 00'	485	Entrance of Denmark Strait.
83:	62° 25'	28° 30'	912	Somewhat more to the North.
84:	62° 58'	25° 24'	633	Denmark Strait.
91:	64° 44'	31° 00'	1236	Likewise.
95:	65 14'	30° 39'	752	Likewise.
96:	65° 24'	29 00'	735	Likewise.

The depth thus varied, after the trawling journal, from 295 to 1435 fathoms. The bottom-temperatures noted varied from 0°.3 to 6°.1 C. The Ingolf» expeditions never got this species north of the ridges between Greenland and Iceland, and between Iceland and the Faroe-Islands. On most of the enumerated stations there was fished with vertical nets too, reaching to a depth of 100--200 fath. without any *Cyclothone* being caught, although small fishes and young ones were taken.

Cyclothone (?) megalops n. sp. ad int. (Table 4, fig. 6).

Together with a great number of *Cyclothone microdon* captured at Station 12 — 64° 38' Lat. N., 32 37' Long. West, 1040 fathoms — there occurred a single specimen of a length of 70ᵐᵐ, habitually looking much like the said species, but differring by the eyes not being particularly small and by totally wanting the light-glands or «photospheres». It can therefore apparently hardly be referred to the same genus. The dorsal and anal fins are very like those of *C. microdon*, though with the difference that the dorsal fin begins somewhat before the anal fin, while this on the other hand ends somewhat farther back than the dorsal fin. Quite black. — A somewhat larger specimen (105ᵐᵐ) from Station 9 — 64 18′ Lat. North and 27° Long. W., 295 fathoms — is so badly preserved, that it gives only the information that the eyes are not small and that both jaws are armed with small teeth directed obliquely backwards, with a few longer ones in the foremost part of the lower jaw and the foremost part of the palate or the intermaxillary. The nearer determination of this specimen must be reserved for a future discovery.

It seems evident that these specimens belong to species else unknown, but as the material is so scanty I shall limit myself to the short preliminary notes made above.

The Notacanths.

For a long time, only few specimens of the remarcable group, the *Notacanthini*, were known of the type termed *Campylodon* (Bugtetanden) by Otto Fabricius (Skrifter af Naturhistorie Selskabet, Vol. IV, fasc. II (1798), p. 22—38, pl. 9, fig. 1), but inserted in the system as *Notacanthus Chemnitzii* Bl. (Abhandlungen der böhmischen Gesellschaft, 1787) or as *Notacanthus nasus* Bl. (Ausländische Fische, IX, Allgemeine Naturgeschichte der Fische, XII, p. 113 (1793), pl. 431); Schneider, «Systema ichthyologiæ (1801), pl. 77. The older Reinhardt designated it in his «Ichthyologiske Bidrag» (Vidensk. Selsk. Skr. VII) p. 120 as *Campylodon Fabricii*, but now-a-days it is generally better known as *Notacanthus nasus*. These few specimens are 1) The original Greenland specimen of Fabricius, which, it must be deplored, in the course of time has been lost — I can not say at what time. 2) The specimen received by Bloch from Chemnitz, probably from Iceland, though it was stated to come «from India». It is described and figured in Cuvier's and Valenciennes's «Histoire naturelle des poissons» VIII, p. 467, pl. 241. It is still preserved, as has been stated subsequently, in the Berlin-Museum in a rather deteriorated condition. 3) A third large specimen was received at our museum in 1871 from Greenland; it is mentioned and partly described by me in 1878 in the «Videnskabelige Meddelelser fra den naturhistoriske Forening». 4) The specimen obtained from Iceland for the Museum of Paris on the voyage of «la Recherche» or rather as a consequence of this voyage (Gaimard: Voyage en Islande et au Grönland, Poissons, pl. XI); Vaillant mentions this specimen (Expéditions scientifiques p. 316) as being from «Greenland», but that is not correct. It is figured twice in the édition illustrée du «Règne animal» de Cuvier (Poissons pl. 55, fig. 2) and in the above quoted itinerary by Gaimard. The question if these 4 arctic specimens should perhaps represent more than a single species did not attract the attention for a long time to come. But now some Mediterranean species were discovered: *Not. Bonapartii* Risso (Archiv für Naturgeschichte 1840, p. 376; Mem. Acad. d. Sc. Torino, t. XVIII, p. 190) and *N. mediterraneus* Fil. & Verany (Mem. Acad. d. Sc.

Torino, t. XVIII, p. 187; Vaillant: Recherches scientifiques etc. p. 325, pl. 27, fig. 2). Further an Australian species (N. sexspinis Richardson, ‹Voyage of H. M. ships Erebus and Terror , Fishes p. 54, pl. 32, fig. 4 –11; described and figured again in Günther's ‹Report on deep-sea fishes› (Challenger) p. 243, pl. 60, fig. 9 15 and pl. 61, fig. A). Then, in deeper water on the eastern side of North America were found 2 species: N. analis (Gill: Proceedings United States National Museum, VI (1883, p. 255) and N. phasganorus (Goode: Proc. Un. St. Nat. Museum, III (1882), p. 435, ‹Oceanic Ichthyology› p. 167, fig. 186). The question did now arise, if the individual or specific variation had not been supposed to be larger than it is in reality, and if not one or some of the arctic specimens enumerated above could be referred to the species established by the American authors. Léon Vaillant has expressed the opinion that the Icelandic specimens from ‹la Recherche could be referred to N. phasganorus Goode. My own earlier studies of the material at hand or described elsewhere induced me to conclude that the then known Icelandic or Greenlandian specimens should be determined as N. nasus. According to Mr. Bean and Goode (Oceanic Ichthyology p. 166) N. Bonapartii and N. mediterraneus should not be different, but some authors are of the opinion, that the species from the westcoast of South America designated with one of these names (N. Bonapartii, Günthers Report› etc. p. 249, tab. 61, fig. C) is a proper species and genus, now termed Gigliolia Moselcyi (Oceanic Ichthyology› p. 169, fig. 187, 193).

To quite another type belongs a Notacanthus of the subgenus Polyacanthonotus Gthr. and of the particular subdivision termed Macdonaldia, brought home by Ingolf s expedition in 1895. The species has already been described twice by Collett (Diagnoses de poissons nouveaux provenant des campagnes de l'Hirondelle›: Bulletin de la Société zoologique, 1883, p. 307; and Résultats des campagnes scientifiques par Albert Iᵉʳ, prince souverain de Monaco, pars X, Poissons provenant des campagnes du yacht l'Hirondelle , 1896, p. 48, pl. 5, fig. 21) and by Brown Goode & Tarleton Bean (A revision of the order Heteromi, deep-sea fishes, with a description of the new generic types Macdonaldia and Lipogenys, Proc. Unit. Stat. National Museum t. 17 (1894), p. 455, pl. 18, fig. 2; ‹Oceanic Ichthyology» p. 171 pl. 51, fig. 189 and pl. 52, fig. 195). Of other species belonging to the same type are known the Mediterranean N. rissoanus (Filippi & Verany: Mem. Acad. Sc. Torino, t. XVIII, p. 190; Vaillant: ‹Expéditions scientifiques» p. 335, pl. 27, fig. 1, coast of Marocco, 2212 metres) and the Japan form, designated by Günther (Report on deep-sea fishes p. 250, pl. 61, fig. B; Vaillant l. c. p. 387) under the same name, but to which Vaillant and the oft mentioned American scientists now agree to apply a new name (N. Challengeri Vaill.).

As Polyacanthonotus (Macdonaldia) rostratus Coll. is new for the ocean bespoken here the Ingolfian specimen deserves to be mentioned in a more particular fashion. As in the related species the body is elongate, somewhat compressed and tapers to a rather flagelliform caudal portion; the head is small and terminates in a soft, somewhat pointed snout. The total length to the point of the caudal fin is 355ᵐᵐ; the greatest hight (over the anus) c. 29ᵐᵐ, approximatively $^1/_{12}$ of the total length (the specimen described by Collett was 480ᵐᵐ, the tail being 275ᵐᵐ, the greatest height 37ᵐᵐ, the length of the head 46ᵐᵐ). The distance from the point of the snout to the anus is 120ᵐᵐ, or about $^1/_3$ of the total length, that of the tail the double of the length of the head and the trunk taken together or $^2/_3$ of the whole. The eyes are small, their diameter and the distance between them being 5ᵐ·ⁿ or $^1/_8$

of the length of the head (to the posterior border of the gill-cover); the length of the snout from the eye to the point of the snout is 13^{mm} or $^1/_3$ of the total length of the head, from the mouth to the point of the snout about the half (6^{mm}); the mouth is small, semilunar in shape and situated on the lower side of the snout, the corners of the mouth are vertically below the anterior nostrils. The nostrils are placed close together before the eye. The teeth are fine. The upper jaw ends posteriorly with a rather strong spine.

The pectoral fins have a length of 18^{mm}; their rays are 14. The ventral fins number 10 rays, none of which can be termed a spinous ray, the external one being however thin and delicate. The row of spinous dorsal rays begins exactly over the posterior border of the branchiostegal membrane; it numbers 33 spinous rays (the specimen of Collett had 27, that of Goode & Bean 28—31, *N. Challengeri* 34, *N. rissoanus* 37), they are short and isolated, their mutual distance somewhat surpassing their length, but they become longer and more distant from each other posteriorly: the connecting dermal part is very slight. The spinous rays of the anal fin are also short, but nevertheless much longer than those of the dorsal fin, and they are much more closely approximated to each other than the dorsals. As they approach to the soft rayed portion the connecting dermal skin becomes more distinct. The number of these spinous rays can be reckoned to be about 45 (in Collett's specimen 53, in that of Goode and Bean it is given as 42—53; in *N. Challengeri* 54, in *N. rissoanus* 27), but an absolute limit can not be drawn between the spinous and the soft-rayed part of the fin, when the rays, preserving their undivided shape, become longer, more delicate, articulate and united with a full fin-membrane. The number of rays in this anal fin may be counted as about 190 (perhaps 192—93). In the last part of the tail the hight of the anal fin considerably exceeds that of the tail itself. A caudal fin of 4 rays may be pointed out.

The scales are very delicate. A distinct lateral line may be traced forwards from a point under the last spinous dorsal ray but three; after this point it is less distinct, and is likewise becomes indistinct towards the eye, but reappears then distinctly as an infraorbital line. On the trunk proper its position is nearer to the back than to the belly, but as the body decreases in height its position becomes nearer to the middle height of the body. On the snout are seen several pores, especially a distinct series of such along the inferior margin of the preopercle and of the lower jaw. The colour is a light chocolate colour, somewhat spotted, the opercle is internally black, pellucid towards the margin; also the lips; the inferior portion of the anal fin is also relatively dark.

Our only specimen of this *Polyacanthonotus* or *Macdonaldia* was taken at a depth of 362 fathoms on station **35** (65° 16′ Lat. North, 55° 05′ Long. West). The bottom was a brownish mud with arenaceous foraminifera and pebbles; the temperature was 3°.6 C. The specimen of the prince of Monaco was taken off Newfoundland on a depth of 1267 metres, those of Goode and Bean at 551 and 563 fathoms, at 39° 47—48′ Lat. North and 70° 30—36′ Long. West. The vertical distribution may therefore be fixed provisionally at 360—960 fathoms, the geographical distribution to the western part of the Atlantic from Newfoundland to the Baffin Bay.

Cyclopteridæ and Liparididæ.

Cyclopterus (Eumicrotremus) spinosus (Fabr.).

Of this well-known arctic species the ‹Ingolf›-Expedition has brought home a young specimen captured southwest of Sukkertoppen on station **33**, 67° 57′ Lat. North, 55° 30′ Long. West, at 35 fathoms, sandy bottom, with a bottom-temperature of 0°.8 C.

The species is known from Greenland, Norway, Iceland and Spitsbergen and from some parts of the east coast of America (Oceanic Ichthyology p. 272) and from the Bering-Sea as *Cyclopterus orbis* Gthr. (Catal. Fishes III, p. 158). It is also noted in Gilbert's paper of 1896 on the north-pacific fishes (p. 448) with a note that the identity of *C. orbis* and *C. spinosus* ought to be confirmed through the confrontation of both types, while *C. orbis* is named without any further remark in Jordan and Starks's The fishes of Puget Sound‹ (1895) p. 829 (Leland Stanford jun. University publications, Proceedings of the California Academy of Sciences, Series II, vol. V).

Liparis Reinhardti and L. micropus Gthr.

Those, who may have consulted my little paper of 1886 on the *Liparidæ* (‹Dijmphna expedition) or that of Collett from 1880 (Norske Nordhavs Expedition), will be aware, that the results arrived at by us with respect to the northern Liparids were generally the following. We know 1) a *Liparis Montagui* Don. and 2) a *Liparis lineatus* (Lepechin), both of which make their appearance in unicoloured, spotted and striated varieties, the latter type perhaps identical as species with *L. tunicatus* and to be considered as a minor variety or stage of evolution of the arctic form, which can attain a considerable size and be furnished with a sort of small corneous tubercles or scales. 3) *Liparis Fabricii* Kr. (with the variety *L. leprosa* m.), best known from the Kara-Sea, determined after an original specimen of Kroyer's species, but after my opinion not to be identified with *L. tunicatus*, as it will be seen has been done. 4) *L. Reinhardti* Kr., regarded by several as type for a particular genus (*Careproctus*), what I do not find necessary, but further identified with *L. gelatinosus* Pall., perhaps correctly, though I can not take upon me the responsibility of his identification.

The result arrived at by F. Smitt in his great and handsome work on the ‹Fishes of Scandinavia does not differ much, but somewhat from that exposed above. He has 1) a *Cyclogaster Montagui*; 2) a *C. liparis*, comprising a) as ‹forma microps› the varieties *C. lineatus, vulgaris, barbatus* and *tunicatus*, b) as *forma megalops*‹ my *L. Fabricii*; 3) *C. gelatinosus* Pall. 2: *L. (Careproctus) Reinhardti*, to which *Liparis (Careproctus) micropus* Gthr. perhaps also must be reckoned as a synonym.

I shall add a review, as short as possible, of the further and extra-Scandinavian development of the *Liparis*-question. Garman's monograph of the *Discoboli (Cyclopteridæ, Liparopsidæ* and *Liparididæ)* (Memoirs of the Museum of Comparative Zoology at Harvard College vol. XIV, No. 2) distinguishes first a division, *Cyclopteridæ* with the genera and species: *Cyclopterus (lumpus), Eumicrotremus (spinosus* and *orbis)* and *Cyclopteroides gyrinops*. The last mentioned type from St. Paul's Island (Alaska) is distinguished partly by the position of small barbels along the margin of the lower jaw (cp. the figures t. XI, fig. 4—9; p. 37 it is said in a less definite manner: ‹chin with tubular pores, or barbels). The second division *Liparopsidæ* comprises *Cyclopterichthys ventricosus* (Pallas) [identified with the *Cyclopterus glaber* of Steindachner (Ichthyologische Beiträge X, p. 14, pl. 8) from Kamschatka and the sea of Okotsh] and *Cyclopterus amissus* Vaillant (Strait of Magellan, Mission scientifique du Cap Horn p. 33) and *Liparops Stelleri* (Pallas). Among the true *Liparidialæ* are mentioned of the genus *Liparis* 1) *L. Montagui* (t. VII, fig. 6—20 and VIII, fig. 8—11) with several synonyms from European and Eastamerican places 2) *L. mucosus* Ayr. (Tab. V, fig. 1—5, Tab. IX, fig. 1, Tab. X, fig. A) (California, Alaska etc.); 3) *L. calliodon* (Pall.) identified with *L. cyclopus* Gthr.) (t. VI, fig. 1—5) (Kamschatka); 4) *L. liparis* L. (= *L. lineatus* Lepech., Kr.), *L. vulgaris* Fl., *L. barbatus* Ekst. (from European and American seas) Tab. VII, fig. 1—5, 21, 22; 5) *L. antarctica* Putn. (t. VI, fig. 6—10), according to Gill an *Enantioliparis* (southmost part of Southamerica). To the genus or subgenus *Careliparis* is referred 1) *C. liparis* Bl. Cuv. (= *L. gibbus* Beau) (tab. I—III) (Behring's-Strait etc.), 2) *C. tunicatus* Rhdt. (*L. arctica* Gill, *Fabricii* Kr., *lineatus* Coll. p. p., 3) *C. Steineni* Fischer (*Enantioliparis*, South-Georgia), 4) *L. pulchellus* Ayr. (t. IV, t. V, fig. 6—8, t. VIII, fig. 4—7, 12—14), 5) *L. pallidus* Vaill. (Tierra del Fuego, Missions scientifiques) pl. IV, fig. 3). Under *Careproctus* are noted *C. micropus* Gthr. (Challenger, Report pl. XII, fig. B); the *Gymnolycodes Edwarsii* of Vaillant (Expéditions scientifiques t. 26, fig. 3) is thought perhaps to be the same species, further *C. major* (of which more below) *C. gelatinosus* (Pall.) and *C. Reinhardti*, which is not identified with *C. gelatinosus*, but with *L. ranula* G. & B.

In Oceanic Ichthyology are named, not only *Paraliparis* and the nearest allied apodal types, the so called *Amittrinæ*, 3 genera of true Liparids, viz 1) *Liparis* (Artedi): Expl. *Cyclopterus liparis* L. = *C. lineatus* Lepech., Kr., *L. vulgaris* Fl., *L. barbatus* Ekst. 2) *Careliparis* (compare the monograph of Garman cited above). 3) *Careproctus* Kr., distinguished after the old definition by the ventral disk being small and placed below the head. Further is noted *L. (C.) Reinhardti* Kr., in which some have meant to recognise the *Cyclopterus gelatinosus* of Pallas and which is therefore termed *C. gelatinosus* (Pall.); an allied type is designed *C. spectrum* Bean from Alaska; further a *C. ranula* G. & B. (fig. 251), fished off Halifax, and *C. micropus* Gthr.; and finally a species termed *C. major*, answering to the *Liparis* or *Actinochir major* of the Northamerican ichthyologists (the denomination after the *Cyclopterus liparis var. major* of Fabricius) and identified with the Greenlandian *L. tunicata* and with the *L. Fabricii* described by Kara-Havets Fiske (after my opinion identical with Kroyer's species of the same name, but in no way with *L. tunicatus* Reinhardt). A doubt (well founded I believe) is also expressed, whether this *Liparis* be really a *Careproctus*!

Of other Liparids are named in Jordans and Starks's paper on the fishes of Puget Sound *Neoliparis Floræ* and *N. Greeni*, *N. mucosus* Ayr., *N. callyodon* Pall. (= *L. mucosus* Garm.), *L. cyclopus* Gthr., *L. Dennyi* J. St., *L. fucensis* Gilb. and *L. pulchellus* Ayr. Others are further mentioned in Gilbert's »The ichthyological collections of U. F. C. St. »Albatross« during 1890—91» from the sea off the coast of California: *Careproctus melanurus* G. with the rather important remark, that the disk becomes smaller with age, but that its place like that of the anus remains unaltered. Further are named from Unalaska and Alaska etc. a *Careproctus retenes* Gr., *C. Colleti* G., *C. phasma* G., *C. simus* G., *C. ostentum* Gilb. (the disk reduced to a rudiment), *Gyrinichthys* (n. g.) *minytremus*, *Rhinoliparis* (n. g.) *barbulifer*, *Bathyphasma* (n. g.) *ovigerum* Gilb., *Liparis pulchellus* Ayr., *L. cy-*

clapus Gthr., *L. Agassizi* Putn., *L. cyclostigma* Gilb., *L. fucensis* (-- *L. calliodon*) Garman, *Neoliparis callyodon* Pall. (= *L. mucosus* Garm.), *L. gibbus* Bean.

This synopsis should approximatively illustrate the actual floating condition of this rather hopeless *Liparis* question per tot discrimina rerum.

Some specimens brought home by the Ingolf expedition (generally in a less good condition) from cold and deep water are perhaps better or equally correctly to be termed *L. micropus*. Of the relation between this species and *L. Reinhardti* I shall not give a personal opinion. After the localities they are from

Station	Lat. N.	Long. W.	Fath.	
34:	67 17′	54 17′	55	Sandy bottom, Bottom-temp. 0.9 C. West of Greenland, Davis Strait.
67:	61 30′	22 30′	975	Bottom-temp. 3 C. South of Cape Reykjanæs.
92:	64 44′	32 52′	976	Bottom-temp. 1.4 C. West of Iceland, Denmark Strait.
116:	70 05′	8 26′	371	Brown Biloculina clay, Bottom-temp. ÷0.4 C. South of Jan Mayen.
126:	67 19′	15 52′	293	Grayish brown, blue clayish mud, Bott.-temp. ÷0.5 C. North of Iceland.
141:	63 22′	6 58′	679	Gray mud, Bottom-temp. ÷0.6 C. North of Faroe Islands.

Thus all specimens were from depths or under conditions where the temperature at the bottom was at the highest 3 C. or below (÷0.6).

A large and handsome specimen (Tab. III, fig. 3 and 3a) from the station 139 (63° 36′ Lat. North, 7° 30′ Long. West, depth 702 fathoms, gray clay, bottom-temperature ÷0.6 C.) surpasses in size (270^{mm}) widely every other known specimen of *L. Reinhardti*. I have had it figured with the aid of a coloured sketch made on the Ingolf. The differences, that may be found between this individual and other existing descriptions of *Liparis (Careproctus) Reinhardti (gelatinosus)* should perhaps essentially be attributed to the fact, that with the exception of the original type of Pallas ordinarily only smaller (younger) specimens have been studied, while we here have the rare success to have before us an older, adult specimen. On the other hand I can not deny the possibility that it may be identical with one of the other established *Careproctus*-species, or maintain absolutely its identity with Pallas's *L. gelatinosus*, on which the older Reinhardt had already fixed the attention for the type which at a later time bore his name. The length of the fish is stated above; the length, breadth and the height of the head are 55^{mm}, 45^{mm} and 55^{mm}. The largest height behind the head is 74^{mm}; when it apparently decreases relatively slowly backwards, this appearance is due to the considerable height of the dorsal and anal fins. The transversal breadth of the mouth is 35^{mm}; along the upper jaw and between the nostrils 7 pores are seen, along the lower jaw one and in the continuation thereof 7. A couple of low tubeformed nostrils with a mutual distance of 17^{mm} are seen anteriorly on a line, that would unite the anterior margins of the eyes; their distance from the eyes is 7^{mm}, from the margin of the jaw 12^{mm}. The diameter of the globular eyes is 11^{mm}, their mutual distance 32^{mm} and from the jaws' margin 13^{mm}, the height of the branchial cleft 17^{mm}. The whole number of pectoral rays is 31; the pectorals meet approximately below the head; as in the smaller individuals they get a fringed appearance, the rays continuing beyond the connecting membrane, especially those in the anterior (or undermost) part of the fin, where their free portion may obtain the length of 39^{mm}. The small ventral disk has a diameter of 12^{mm}; it is situated under the centre of the eyes. The dorsal fin numbers c. 40 rays, the caudal fin 10, and the anal fin c. 40 rays.

It will perhaps be useful to print here the following extract of Jordan and Starks's conspectus of the American species of *Liparis* and *Neoliparis* ("The fishes of Puget Sound" p. 837 og 834).

a. *Liparis*: number of vertebræ c. 39; radii dorsales c. 35; radii anales 27—30.
  b. The gill-clefts very narrow, entirely over the base of the pectorals; rad. caudales 12. *L. liparis.*
  bb. The gill-clefts larger, partly below the uppermost pectoral ray.
    c. Radii pectorales 30; rad. caudales 12. *L. cyclopus* (l. c. pl. 97).
    cc. Radii pectorales 41—43; rad. caudales 15—20. *L. fucensis.*
aa. *Careliparis* Garm.: Number of vertebræ c. 46; radii dorsales 40—44; radii anales 35—36.
    d. Radii pectorales 35—36.
      e. Gill-clefts small, not reaching beyond the first pectoral ray.
        f. *L. tunicatus.*
        ff. *L. Agassizii.*
      ee. Gill-clefts large, reaching down to the fourth pectoral ray. *L. Dennyi* (l. c. pl. 98).
    dd. Radii pectorales 42; gill-clefts large, reaching to and beyond the upper part of the pectorals. *L. cyclostigma.*
aaa. *Actinochir*: Number of vertebræ c. 52; radii dorsales 45—48, radii anales 38—40, radii pectorales 34—37.
      g. *A. pulchellus.*
      gg. *A. major.*

Neoliparis.
a. Gill-clefts very narrow, not reaching beyond the third pectoral ray.
  b. Anterior nostril distinctly tubiform.
    c. Radii dorsales c. 30, radii anales 24. *N. montagui.*
    cc. Radii dorsales 34—36, radii anales 25—28. *N. callyodon* Pall. (*L. mucosus* Garm.).
  bb. Anterior nostril not distinctly tubiform. Radii dorsales 32, radii anales 26. *N. mucosus* (l. c. pl. 95).
aa. Gill-clefts relatively large; nostrils not distinctly tubiform.
    d. Radii dorsales VI — 27, radii anales 21—23, radii pectorales 30. *N. floræ* (l. c. pl. 96).
    dd. Radii dorsales VI — 34, radii anales 30, radii pectorales 35. *N. greeni* (l. c. pl. 96).

Paraliparis bathybii (Coll.).

The establishment of this hitherto unknown form was based upon a single specimen, 208^{mm} long, taken on the Norwegian North-Sea-Expedition to the North Sea, on a depth of 568 fathoms, west of Bceren-Island; it wanted the ventrals, and it had at that time to be left in doubt, whether this was a constant deficiency or it was only due to an accident. It was therefore referred to the genus *Liparis* with the annotation, that it would perhaps form a proper genus ("Den norske Nordhavs-Expedition", Fiskene p. 52, t. 2, fig. 14). Then the "British Museum" also received a specimen, 7$^{1}/_{2}$ inches long, fished by the "Knight Errant" on the North-Sea-Expedition of this vessel in the «Faroe Channel» on a depth of 640 fathoms (Challenger, deep-sea fishes p. 68, pl. XII, fig. C). It turned out that it really wanted the ventrals and consequently an adhesive disk, formed by them, but is was not confirmed — what has not been found by me neither — that under the chief portion of the pectoral are found c. 4 rudimentary rays; but it was confirmed, that the pectoral fin did consist apparently of 2 divisions, a greater of 12 rays and a smaller party, divided from the other, of 3 rays. At the same time Goode and Bean described a *P. Copei* G. & B. and a *Imitra* or *Monomitra liparina* Goode, which in Oceanic Ichthyology p. 277 is upheld as a proper genus; the localities where these types are found in the northern Atlantic are noted in the said work, where also sketches of them are given (fig. 252 and 253). Concerning the small *P. membranaceus* Gthr. (Challenger, Report etc. p. 69, pl. 12, fig. D) which in the Oceanic Ichthyology is raised as the type of a proper genus, *Hilgendorfia*, it would be more correct to postpone one's judgement until a larger material is at hand. Finally I shall add, that in the Oceanic Ichthyology is mentioned (in the Appendix p. 525) a *Paraliparis rosaceus* Gilb. from the Pacific, and that M. Gilbert (The ichthyological collections of U. St. F. Comm. St. Albatross 1890-91, 1896) further has described a *P. holomelas*, *ulochir* and *cephalus* from the northern part of the Pacific and a *P. dactylosus* from California.

As M. Collett and Dr. Günther have given a full account of *Paraliparis bathybii* there will be no necessity for occupying myself further with it here. The number of vertebrae is 10 — 54. I shall only give a list of the 6 stations, which have given the 18 more or less well preserved specimens at hand, of which the 2 largest had a length of 185^{mm}. 220^{mm}.

Stat.	Lat. N.	Long. W.	Fath.	Bottom-temp.	Condition of the bottom		
104:	66 23'	7 25'	957	+ 1.4	Light grayish brown mud.	East of Iceland.	1 specimen.
105:	65 34'	7 31'	762	+0.8	Light brown mud.	Likewise.	7 specimens.
111:	67 14'	8 48'	860	+0.9	Brown Biloculina-clay.	Northeast of Iceland.	1 specimen.
117:	69 13'	8 23'	1003	÷ 1	Light Biloculina-clay.	South of Jan Mayen.	6 specimens.
119:	67 53'	10 19'	1010	÷ 1	Light Biloculina-clay.	Between Iceland and Jan Mayen.	1 specim.
140:	63 29'	6 57'	780	+0.9	Gray mud.	North of the Faroe Islands.	2 specimens.

Blenniodei. Ophidini.

Gymnelis viridis Fabr.

Some few specimens were caught on Ingolf 's expedition at localities, S.W. off Sukkertoppen, viz:

Station	Lat. N.	Long. W.	Fathoms		
29:	65 34'	54 31'	68	Davis Strait. Sandy bottom,	Temperature at the bottom 0°.2 C.
34:	67 17'	54 17'	55	Davis Strait.	Temperature at the bottom 0°.9 C.

In the Denmark Strait it is previously taken at a depth of 80 fathoms.

The largest Ingolfian specimen is 136^{mm}. The ornamental markings, which concist of lighter and darker transversal bands are on the whole not strong. Some of the specimens have 1, 2 or 3 dark spots on the foremost part of the dorsal fin.

The Norwegian North-Sea Expedition got 4 specimens north of Jan Mayen and Spitsbergen, where it also has been found earlier; it is also known from the east coast of Greenland, f. i. Heklas port at a slight depth (the expedition of Ryder). It has also been found in the Kara-Sea and in Barents-Sea and in the arctic part of the Pacific (Unalaska, at a depth of 49 fathoms).

Lumpenus lampetræformis Walb.

is the only northern *Lumpenus*-species brought home in few specimens from a locality Southwest of Sukkertoppen, Station **34**: 67° 17′ Lat. North, 54° 17′ Long. West, depth 55 fathoms, temperature at the bottom 0°.9 C. The largest specimen had a length of 190^{mm}. On the distribution of the species may be consulted Collett, Lilljeborg, and Oceanic Ichthyology.

Flounders.

Drepanopsetta (Hippoglossoides) platessoides (Fabr.).

Of this Pleuronectoid the 'Ingolf expedition has returned some specimens from

Stat.	Lat. N.	Long. W.		Fathoms	
26:	63° 57′	52° 41′	Davis Strait.	34	Bottom sand and shells, temperature 0°.6 C.
33:	67° 57′	55° 30′	Likewise.	35	Bottom gray sand, its temperature 0°.8 C.
35:	65° 16′	55° 05′	Likewise.	362	Bottom brownish mud with arenaceous foraminiferes, tp. 3°.6 C.

known with us as «Haa-Isingen», identical with *Pleuronectes limandoides*, not only from Greenland, also from Iceland, Beeren-Island, Spitsbergen, the Faroe Islands and along the Scandinavian and the Northeuropean shores, from the Murmanian coasts and East-Finmark to the Sound, at Kiel and the southern Danish seas and also from the English-French channel; on the American side to Cape Cod.

The genus *Lycodes*.

It will be well known to the ichthyologists, especially to those studying the arctic fauna, that to distinguish between the species of this genus is connected with special difficulties, because the colouring varies much in the same species, especially after the age, but also individually, likewise the extension of the squamation, and it is therefore extremely difficult to fix the limit between the species by means of characters that may be confided on. As our museum possesses now more or fewer specimens of 15 *Lycodes*-species from the Polar sea, the northern part of the Atlantic[1]) and the Californian part of the Pacific one should hope, that the difficulties might be overcome. But nevertheless my report specially for this department must be given with a certain restraint. The scientific literature amply testifies, that it is a more easy matter to make mistakes in this department than to avoid them. A greater lucidity will not be obtained until the collected material has attained a completeness that at present is only obtained for a few species among the many.

[1]) As this genus was not found formerly in any of the Danish seas, it should be remarked that a fish of this genus, 155^{mm} long, was taken in 1893 in Læsø Rende, afterwards several in the Skager-Rack (jfr. S. 21) viz a *Lycodes gracilis* M. Sars.

Lycodes muræna Coll.

A specimen 10³₄ inches long (275ᵐᵐ) was obtained in the Davis Strait between Godthaab and Sukkertoppen, at Station **27**: 64 54′ Lat. N., 55 10′ Long. W., at a depth of 393 fathoms (a temperature of 3 .8 C. at the bottom, which consisted of a soft gray clay with numerous pebbles, mostly granite). It agrees substantially with the figure and description of Collett (Den norske Nordhavsexpedition , Fiskene, p. 116, pl. IV, fig. 29 31; compare also F. Smitt: Skandinaviens Fiskar p. 618 and Günther's Deep-Sea Fishes: Challenger Expedition S. 79, tab. 12, fig. A). The species has been taken in several instances by the said Norwegian expedition at the banks off Helgeland, Beeren-Island and Spitsbergen (Norsk-Oerne) on depths of 350—658 fathoms, the bottom brown, green or bluish-gray clay, the bottom temperature being + o .9 à ÷ 1 .2 C. *L. muræna* is further taken by an English expedition in the Faroe-channel at 540-608 fathoms. In 1896 Ingolf obtained further 12 younger specimens at the following stations:

Station	Lat. N.	Long. W.		Fathoms	Bottom temp.
65:	61 33′	19	South of Iceland.	1089	3 C.
102:	66 23′	10 26′	East of Iceland.	750	÷ o .9 C.
104:	66 23′	7 25′	Likewise.	957	÷ 1 .1 C.
105:	65 34′	7 31′	Likewise.	762	÷ o .8 C.
117:	69 13′	8 23′	South of Jan Mayen.	1003	÷ 1 C.
125:	68 08′	16 02′	North of Iceland.	729	+ o .8 C.
139:	63 36′	7 30′	North of Faroe Islands.	702	÷ o .6 C.

The larger specimen from Stat. **27**, the only squamate, has larger eyes than the smaller and younger ones, apparently also a less flattish head and a shorter snout. It is therefore not quite certain that it is identical as species with these. The size of the younger specimens lies between 203ᵐᵐ and 108ᵐᵐ. Of the scales nothing is seen in these smaller specimens. In the larger of them the length of the head is scarcely ¹⁄₅ of that of the whole body (trunk and tail), in the smaller ones it varies between 1 ÷6.5 and 1 ÷8.1. With 2 exceptions (Stat. 27 and **65**, where the bottom temperature was 3 .8 and 3) all these specimens were from stations with a bottom temperature below zero.

Of allied species with a similar longish eel-like shape some other species are described 1) *L. Verrillii* G. & B., 2) *L. paxillus* G. & B. (into which *L. paxilloides* is afterwards drawn as a synonym), for these species may be consulted the Oceanic Ichthyology p. 309 11 and 527, fig. 277. 279, 280 and 282. Further 3) *L. (Lycodonus) mirabilis* Goode & Bean (Günther: Deep-Sea Fishes, Challenger Report etc. p. 81); 4) *L. (Lycodophis) albus* Vaill. (Expéditions scientifiques du Travailleur p. 309, pl. 26, fig. 11, caught at a depth of 3975 metres on the way between the Azores and France, and 5) *L. (Lysenchelys) porifer* Gilb. (Proceed. Un. St. Nat. Mus. XIII (1890), p. 104), from South California at a depth of 857 fathoms.

Lycodes frigidus Coll.

Den norske Nordhavs Expedition , Fiskene, p. 96, pl. III, fig. 24; Oceanic Ichthyology p. 335, fig. 274.

As I have no doubt that the numerous specimens of a *Lycodes*, taken in larger or smaller specimens in the eastern part of the North Sea, at the stations enumerated below, belong to the said species, which is carefully described and excellently figured in the Norwegian work cited here, I shall limit myself to a few remarks. As characteristic for *L. frigidus* may be mentioned the uniform dark or brownish colour and the uniform delicate squamation on the entire body to the occiput and the branchial orifice and on the belly. Further the lateral-ventral side-line, starting from the upper end of the branchial orifice, then arches downwards, running parallel with the lower margin of the tail in a great extent. Young specimens (until 110^{mm} length) are entirely naked, in the somewhat greater ones the scales cover a smaller or larger part of the tail, and in the more mature state of the fish they spread over the trunk and the belly.

The Ingolfian specimens are from the following stations.

Stat.	Lat. N.	Long. W.		Fathoms	Condition of the bottom	Bottom temp.
102:	66° 23'	10 26'	East of Iceland.	750	Brown mud	÷ 0 .9 C.
104:	66° 23'	7 25'	Likewise.	957	Light grayish brown mud	÷ 1°.1 C.
110:	66° 44'	11° 33'	Likewise.	781	Brown mud	÷ 0°.8 C.
111:	67° 14'	8° 48'	Northeast of Iceland.	860	Brown mud	+ 0 .9 C.
112:	67° 57'	6 44'	Likewise.	1267	Biloculina-clay	÷ 1 .1 C.
113:	69° 31'	7° 06'	South of Jan Mayen.	1309	Biloculina-clay	÷ 1 .0 C.
117:	69 13'	8 23'	Likewise.	1003	Light Biloculina-clay	÷ 1°.0 C.
118:	68° 27'	8 20'	Likewise.	1060	Light Biloculina-clay	+ 1 .0 C.
119:	67 53'	10 19'	Between Iceland and Jan Mayen.	1010	Light Biloculina-clay	÷ 1°.0 C.
120:	67 29'	11 32'	Northeast of Iceland.	885	Light Biloculina-clay	÷ 1 .0 C.
124:	67 40'	15 40'	North of Iceland.	495	Brownish gray blue mud with short arenaceous foraminifera	÷ 0 .6 C.
125:	68° 08'	16 02'	North of Iceland.	729	Brown mud	÷ 0°.8 C.

The largest specimen of the »North-Sea Expedition» has a length of little more than half a meter; a specimen of a little larger size in the »Ingolf -collection reminds so much of the *L. reticulatus* Gthr. (Challenger Expedition p. 77, pl. XIII), that I must regard them as absolutely identical. The specimens of the »North-Sea Expedition» were from the seas around Beeren Island and Spitsbergen. From the American expeditions of the »Albatross« a series of localities is indicated (»Oceanic Ichthyology« l. c.).

Lycodes Esmarkii (Coll., l. c. p. 84, pl. II, fig. 19 21 and pl. III, fig. 22).

A specimen, 260^{mm} in length, from Station 138: North of the Faroe Islands (63° 26' Lat. North, 7° 56' Long. West, depth 471 fathoms, temperature at the bottom ÷ 0°.6 C.) having 5 light bands over the dorsal fin and the back and with both a medio-lateral and a ventro-lateral lateral line, agreeing well with Colletts fig. 21, represents this type in the collections of »the Ingolf«. Previously known from the banks off Lofoten and from the north-west coast of Spitsbergen and from several points of Finmarken (260 459 fathoms).

Lycodes Lütkenii Coll. (l. c. p. 103, pl. III, fig. 25).

Is likewise taken formerly west of North-Spitsbergen (459 fathoms) and in the Kara sea. The Ingolf Expedition got 6 specimens from station 116: South of Jan Mayen (70° 05′ Lat. North, 8° 26′ Long. W.), depth 371 fathoms, temperature at the bottom ÷ 0°.4 C. The coloration is essentially as in the specimen figured by Collett: 6–8 light bands.

Lycodes perspicillum Kr. (*L. reticulatus* Rhdt. juv.?). (Tab. IV, fig. 5.)

A young (42ᵐᵐ) specimen of this species with the characteristic dress of many young Lycodidæ a series of 10 darkly bordered saddle-spots across the back was fished on sandy bottom off Sukkertoppen, Davis Strait (Station 29), 64° 34′ Lat. N., 54° 31′ Long. W., at a depth of 68 fathoms.

L. gracilis Sars.

To this species, after having conferred with my colleague, Prof. Collett, I have referred two specimens from station 31: Davis Strait (66° 35′ Lat. North, 55° 54′ Long. West, depth 88 fathoms, temperature at the bottom 1°.6 C.) They are 5¹⁄₂ and 9¹⁴ inches long, both covered with scales. The relation between the length of the head with the trunk and the entire length (100ᵐᵐ ÷ 244ᵐᵐ and 55ᵐᵐ ÷ 143ᵐᵐ) is about 1 ÷ 2¹ ₂ à 2¹ ₂. In colour they are light with more or less distinct traces of the juvenile dress.

L. gracilis was known from a small specimen (43ᵐᵐ) from the Christiania Fjord (Nordhavs Expeditionen p. 106) and is later found again in Læso Rende and in the Skager Rack in adult specimens. I suppose that Prof. Collett will give a full account of the species in its more developed condition as it is now known.

L. pallidus Coll.

(Nordhavs-Expeditionen p. 110, pl. III, fig. 26, 27; Lütken: ‹Kara Havets Fiske› p. 134, pl. 17, fig. 1–3.)

Of this species there are from the Ingolf -Expedition:

Station	Lat. N.	Long. W.	Fathoms	Temp. at the bottom	
101:	66° 23′	12 05′	537	+ 0°.7 C.	East of Iceland.
104:	66° 23′	7 25′	957	÷ 1°.1 C.	
105:	65° 34′	7 31′	762	÷ 0°.8 C.	
116:	70 05′	8 26′	371	+ 0°.4 C.	South of Jan Mayen.
124:	67 40′	15 40′	495	÷ 0 .6 C.	North of Iceland.
126:	67° 19′	15° 52′	293	÷ 0 .5 C.	
138:	63 26′	7° 56′	471	÷ 0°.6 C.	North of the Faroe Islands.
141:	63 22′	6° 58′	679	+ 0°.6 C.	

Hitherto known from the northern coast of Spitsbergen, 260–458 fathoms (Collett) and from the Kara sea (Lütken). The specimens from the ‹Ingolf expedition have a size reaching to 245ᵐᵐ. The larger specimens are scaled on the belly and uniformly light brown without marks of transverse bands or design on the fins, the smaller have bands on the fins and partly on the body, but want the scales on the belly.

Note. It will perhaps be useful to resume how matters stand at present with the synonymy of the species of *Lycodes* named here. *L. reticulatus* is founded by the older Reinhardt ("Forste Bidrag til Gronlands ichthyologiske Fauna" p. 167, t. VI) on specimens from Greenland. Collett (l. c. p. 84) refers to the same species the following descriptions: *L. polaris* Ross. (Spitsbergen), *L. polaris* Mlmgr. (Ofvers. Vet. Akad. Förh. 1864, p. 516) likewise from Spitsbergen, *L. perspicillum* Kr. (from Greenland) and *L. gracilis* Sars (from Christianiafjord). In his great work "Skandinaviens Fiskar" F. Smitt draws the limits of this species still wider, embracing under it not only the type: Reinhardt's *L. reticulatus* and Günther's of the same name ("Challenger" p. 77, pl. XIII; which after my opinion as stated above is a large *L. frigidus* Coll.!) and the type described by me under the same name from the Kara Sea ("Dijmphna" T. 17, fig. 4—5) as also the *L. perspicillum* of Krøyer (regarded also by Collett and myself as a *L. reticulatus*), but also *L. seminudus* Reinhardt from Greenland and Spitsbergen), by Collett (l. c. p. 113, t. IV, f. 28) upheld as a proper species and further *L. Lütkenii* Coll. (l. c. p. 103, t. 111, fig. 25) a name adopted by me for fishes from the Kara Sea ("Dijmphna" p. 128, T. 16, fig. 1—6); and further Beans *L. Turneri* from Alaska (Proc. Un. St. Mus. I, 463), and *L. coccineus* (l. c. IV, p. 144) and my *L. pallidus* ("Dijmphna" p. 134, t. 17, fig. 1—3) and finally *L. mucosus* Rich. (Belcher p. 362, t. 26) the type of Blecker's genus *Lycodalepis*. Of these supposed synonyma the authors of "Oceanic Ichthyology" only cite the "*L. perspicillum* Kr.", "*L. Rossii*" Mlgr. and "*L. gracilis* Sars" to *L. reticulatus*, while they notwithstanding cite (p. 307) a "*L. perspicillum* Kr." as a peculiar type found by the "Albatross" on depths of 59 and 86 fathoms (45°24'30" Lat. North, 58 35'15" Long. West and on 47 29' Lat. North, 25 18' Long. West). It must also be noted that "*L. mucosus*", formerly only known from the description and picture by Belcher "Last of Arctic Voyages" (Northumberland Sound, afterwards found again in Cumberland Sound) is now described and figured in "Oceanic Ichthyology" (p. 306, t. 78, fig. 273 and t. 81, fig. 283, a, b) after a specimen 17 inches long from Northumberland Sound. In the work cited are not mentioned the species of Bean, mentioned by Smitt (*L. Turneri* and *L. coccineus*; the one being from Alaska, the other from "Big Diomede Island"). I shall further add, that the later paper by H. Gilbert ("The ichthyological collections of the U. S. F. Comm. St. Albatross", 1896), containing "Report of the fishes collected in Bering Sea and the North Pacific Ocean during the summer of 1890", describes and figures several new genera and species of the *Lycodes* tribe, while some other species of Gilbert are named, whose original descriptions are not known to me at present. For me and my collaborator it has been a relief in our task, that the "Ingolfian" species were well known to us from Scandinavian ichthyological works.

The *Macrurus* group.

It is well known, that no other group of fishes has received such an accession through the deep-sea-investigations as the Macruridæ (=Skolæsts» or «Berglax» as they are termed in Scandinavia). They were known in 1872 in 10 - 11 species; in the report of the «Challenger expedition» their number is grown to 47, including the species fished by the Northamerican expeditions and published at that period; the French expeditions have added 9—10 species, the Indian 12. Counting the species cited in the Oceanic Ichthyology · I arrive at the number 80, by American and other ichthyologists it is later increased to 94 or more. Through the two «Ingolf» expeditions there are collected 6 species at least. The difficulty to distinguish species, which after all are very nearly similar, is augmented by the alterations undergone with age by the individuals. My task has been relieved by the «Smithsonian Institution» having in the most benevolent manner placed at my disposal 5 species of duplicates from the American fishings. But there is one difficulty, which is still hardly overcome, viz., to get the large material of c. 100 described species distributed in good genera and subgenera in a satisfying manner. Provisionally I may refer to the list of genera in Oceanic Ichthyology , where 17 genera (or subgenera?) are recognised, to which may be added an 18th, later proposed (*Coelocephalus* Gilbert & Cramer). Until further information I retain the name *Macrurus* as a common name for all the arctic and subarctic species here mentioned.

Macrurus Fabricii Sundev. (*rupestris* Fabr. non Gunn.).

The name *M. berglax* Lac. which has been substituted in later times for this species is less convenient for this form, so well known in Greenland, as one will more easily understand it as alluding to the *M. (Coryphænoides) Stromii*, the Berglax of the Norwegians. The largest Ingolfian specimen has a length of 21 inches, it has therefore not the full size of the species; the smallest is only 4½ inches. The stations and localities where they were taken, are

Station	Lat. N.	Long. W.	Fathoms	Temp. of the bottom	
27:	64° 54′	55 10′	393	3°.8 C.	
32:	66° 35′	56° 38′	318	3°.9 C.	all from the Davis Strait.
35:	65° 16′	55 05′	362	3°.6 C.	
38:	59° 12′	51 05′	1870	1°.3 C.	

These localities are partly from the Davis Strait, West of Holsteinsborg and Sukkertoppen, partly from the entrance to the Davis Strait. What shortly can be said of the distribution of the species outside this region is, that it is known more southward, from George's Bank, from the port of New York, were it was found floating at the surface, and from 41° 47′ Lat. North, 65° 37′ 30″ Long. West at a depth of 677 fathoms, and further from the eastern part of the North Sea, the Finnish and Norwegian coasts.

The characters which make this species recognisable are the obtuse shape of the head, the rounded snout, the large eyes whose diameter is the double or more of the breadth of the front between them and equal with or larger than the length of the snout from its points to the orbital margin, the numerous keels along the sides of the trunk and tail, the back and belly, produced by every scale having a strong denticulate keel; on large specimens there is commonly only one such keel, but the greater scales of the head have commonly more (3, 4 or 5) such keels, diverging from forwards backwardly. These larger scales form partly more prominent groups on the opercles and preopercles, partly rows especially on the median line of the snout, round the orbits, along the lower lateral margin of the head etc. A larger naked spot before the eyes gives room for the nostrils; before these there is in larger specimens a smaller naked spot on each side, close to the point of the snout. Below the inferior lateral margin bespoken the skin is naked or only covered with smaller asperities, and the same is the case with the two branches of the lower jaw. In half-grown specimens it is evident, that on the ordinary scales there are besides the chief keel several more or less distinctly serrated accessory keels, 1, 3 or 4 on each side of the chief keel; but the distinct and numerous larger longitudinal keels along the sides of the body are nevertheless equally characteristic for younger and for older specimens. In the very youngest specimens the extension of the scale-covering is more limited   on the belly to the region before the ventrals, while the belly proper is entirely without scales. The shape of the snout is here the same as in other *Macruri*, not bowlike rounded, but sharply triangular. The first dorsal fin begins immediately over the insertion of the pectorals, which again is in the vertical from the first point of the ventrals. The first longest rays of the ventrals are almost equal with those of the pectorals, but shorter than those of the first dorsal fin. The number of rays is 1 + 11 in this fin, 19 in the pectorals, 8 in the ventrals. The teeth are minute, almost hidden between the papillae of the mouth.

Of the other northern species

Macrurus (Coryphænoides) rupestris Gunn. (M. Stromii Rhdt., norvegicus Nilsson)

(figured in ‹Voyage en Scandinavie , Poissons, pl. 11, in Smitt's Scandinavian fishes, pl. XXVII, A, fig. 2, and in Collett's Poissons provenant des campagnes du yacht l'Hirondelle› (1885—88) 1896, pl. 10, fig. 11) there is also a large number of specimens partly from the same localities, where *M. Fabricii* was caught, f. inst.:

Stat. 27: 64 54′ Lat. N., 55°10′ Long. W., 393 fath., bottom temp. 3°.8 C. }
  35: 65°16′   55 05′   362   3°.6 C. } Davis Strait.

partly from others, f. inst.

Stat. 25: 63°30′ Lat. N., 54° 25′ Long. W., 582 fath., bottom temp. 3°.3 C., Davis Strait.
  41: 61°39′   17 10′   -   1245 --   -   2 .0 C., South of Iceland.

Also two larger specimens from

Stat. 90: 64°45′ Lat. N., 29°06′ Long. W., 568 fath., bottom temp. 4°.4 C., length 485ᵐᵐ }
  - 97: 65 28′   27°39′   450   5 .5 C.,   730ᵐᵐ } Denmark Strait.

Young specimens of *M. rupestris* are captured on the following localities:

Stat. 25: 63°30′ Lat. N., 54° 25′ Long. W., 582 fath., soft blue-clayish mud, bottom temp. 3 .3 C. Davis Strait.
 - 27: 64°54′   55° 10′ --   393 —   soft gray clay, bottom temp. 3°.8 C. Davis Strait.
  40: 62 00′ -   21 36′ --   845 --   dark gray mud, bottom temp. 3°.3 C. South of Iceland.
 - 45: 61°32′   9 43′   643 --   bottom temp. 4°.17 C. West of Faroe Islands.
 - 69: 62°40′   22° 17′   589   mud, bottom temp. 3 .9 C. South of Iceland.
  81: 61°44′ -   27°   485 -   mud, bottom temp. 6°.1 C. }
 -- 83: 62 25′   28 30′   912 -   mud, bottom temp. 3°.5 C. } Southwest of Iceland.

The largest specimen has a length of 28 inches, the smallest of 2¹¹/₁₆ inches. As to the geographical distribution, for which the above cited work of Collett may be referred to, it may be remarked, that beyond the shores of West-Greenland and Norway (from Helgeland to Christianiafjord and Bohuslän) this «Berglax» is known from the sea between Shetland and the Faroe Islands and has several times found its way to the most northern shores of Denmark. In ‹Oceanic Ichthyology› p. 403

other stations are noted from the northwestern Atlantic (The specimens of l'Hirondelle were taken South of Newfoundland).

The head, whose length is contained 5 or somewhat more than 6 times in the total length (in *M. Fabricii* a little more than 4 times) is obtusely rounded, terminating in a small knob in the point of the snout, but without prominent crests or keels with larger scales. In younger specimens the crests of the head may be as it were indicated and the obtusely rounded snout may assume a little more angular figure. The oral orifice reaches to the middle of the eyes or almost to the vertical from their posterior margin in large specimens. The jawteeth are very delicate, placed in a single series. The scales are delicately ciliated, relatively small, but numerous, covering in a very regular manner the head, the body and the tail; the smallest are found on the snout and nearest to the eyes, and this covering reaches to the protrusile part of the jaw, there being no naked or half naked papillous surface at the lower part of the head. Only the throat and the gill-membrane are naked. The naked spot where the nostrils are placed is not so great as in *M. Fabricii*. Of the scales it may further be stated, that they are without keels, but densely covered with spinules without any strong tendency to arrange themselves in transversal rows, but are best said to be arranged in no particular order; the tendency to a serial arrangement is perhaps more distinct in younger individuals. The second dorsal fin, whose anterior rays are very insignificant, begins only at a long distance from the first, about at a line with the points of the pectorals (in younger individuals partly somewhat nearer to the first dorsal), the anal however below or close behind the last rays of the first dorsal, the anus being placed so much forwardly, that there is at most the length of an eye-diameter between the anus and the ventrals. The first ray of the ventrals is very long ($^2/_3$ or $^3/_4$ of or, in younger individuals, equal to the length of the head), therefore reaching far out on the anal, whose rays are relatively strong and well developed. The eyes are great, their diameter is equal to or a little smaller than the distance between the orbita and the point of the snout, but commonly much lesser than $— ^2/_3$ of the frontal breadth. The number of rays is D' 1 + 11, P. 16, V. 8; the first dorsal ray is delicately serrated. The barbel is very small, the lateral line very distinct.

As I have had the opportunity of comparing two half-grown specimens of *Macrurus Bairdii* Goode & Bean (Oceanic Ichthyology p. 393, fig. 335) with *M. Strömii (rupestris)*, I shall - without entering upon a detailed description and perhaps superfluously — observe, that this Northatlantic type is not specifically identical with *M. Strömii* or founded on younger specimens of this — a suspicion that might perhaps offer itself to an ichthyologist not having this opportunity to an immediate comparison.

Macrurus (Hymenocephalus) Goodei Gthr.

(Oceanic Ichthyology p. 407, fig. 340.)

To this species I refer - after comparison with two specimens sent from the Museum at Washington under the names of *Macrurus asper* and *Hymenolaimus Goodei* — the first name being that, under which the species was first described by Goode and Bean, which name however had to be withdrawn, Günther having used it for a Japanese fish — some individuals from the following localities:

Station	Lat. N.	Long. W.		fathoms	temper. of bottom
11:	64 34′	31 12′	(Denmark Strait)	1300	1 .6
36:	61 50′	56 21′	(Davis Strait)	1435	1 .5
37:	60 17′	54 05′	(Davis Strait, at its mouth)	1715	1 .4

From the localities enumerated for *M. Goodei* by Goode and Bean it will be seen that the species is taken so far south as off Havanna, and that the depths noted are between 154 and 1434 fathoms.

The largest specimens have a length of 325^{mm} and 310^{mm}. Their habitus reminds somewhat of that of the *Malacocephali*. The length of the head is contained 5 times or somewhat more in the total length. The diameter of the eyes is somewhat smaller than the diameter of the front and much smaller than the length of the snout. The head is completely scaled with the exception of two parties back of the anterior margin of the snout and an adjoining part of the lower side of the snout. The branchial membrane and the throat are also naked, but the belly proper is scaled like the rest of the head. The scales may be described as ciliate or lineate-ciliate, delicately ribbed with 6 9 scarcely diverging or parallel, low, serrated thorny ribs; the squamification therefore makes a striated impression. The intermaxillary teeth are arranged in two rows, the greater ones in the external row; those of the lower jaw are placed in a single row. The foremost (second) dorsal fin ray, whose point in its depressed condition does not reach to the first low ray of the second dorsal, is serrate anteriorly. The first dorsal has its ordinary place over the ventrals, a little behind the pectorals. The first elongate ray of the pectorals may reach to the anus; the pectorals are not relatively long. The number of the rays are counted thus: D′ 11 + 9; P. 19; V. 9—10. The lateral line is distinct.

Macrurus ingolfi Ltk. sp. n.

Of this apparently hitherto undescribed species 2 specimens (270^{mm} long) are at hand from

Station	Lat. N.	Long. W.		fathoms	temp. at bottom
40:	62 00′	21° 36′	(South of Iceland)	845	3 .3 C.

and one specimen (length: 277—340^{mm}) from each of the following stations:

Station	Lat. N.	Long. W.		fathoms	temp. at bottom
11:	64° 34′	31° 12′	(Denmark Strait)	1300	1 .6 C.
18:	61° 44′	30° 29′	(Southwest of Iceland)	1135	3 .0 C.
64:	62′ 06′	19° 00′	(South of Iceland)	1041	3 .1 C.
83:	62′ 25′	28° 30′	(Southwest of Iceland)	912	3 .5 C.

This species has a considerable likeness with the proceeding species, from which it may be easily distinguished among other things through the larger eyes, the distinct knobs of the snout and a higher first dorsal.

The head is contained about 5 times in the total length. The superior or frontal surface of the snout is separated from the inferior or more forwardly directed part by a well developed crest or edge, terminating in 3 spinose osseous tubercles, one directly in the middle and one on each side, close before the naked spot, where the nostrils have their place, and continued both above and below the

4*

orbita. The broadly triangular snout is prolonged fairly over and before the mouth, which is relatively little, the corners of the mouth falling in a line with the anterior margin or the middle of the orbits. The eyes are large, their diameter surpassing the breadth of the front between the eyes. The teeth form a fine card in both jaws. The head is scaled with the exception of the gill membrane, the isthmus and its foremost superior margin, and almost the whole lower surface. The naked part of the snout is handsomely embroidered with rows of slime glands. The first dorsal counting 11 — 9 rays is singularly high and its longest (second) ray is serrate and as long as the head. The second dorsal begins much forward, its foremost rudimentary rays may be followed until not far from the posterior margin of the first dorsal fin. The pectorals contain 20 rays, and the ventrals, whose external ray tapers to a fine thread and reaches a long stretch beyond the anus have 8 rays. It may also be remarked, that the tail as in other Macrurians is really pointed behind, but in several specimens has lost a shorter or longer part; but the wound has healed, and on the thus truncated point of the tail is developed a distinct caudal fin, a phenomenon which is also observed in some specimens of the proceeding species. The scales show distinct rows of thorns, not however so much projecting as in *M. Goodei*.

Macrurus ingolfi n. sp. differt a *M. Goodei* præcipue oculis majoribus, tuberculis rostralibus magis distinctis et pinna dorsali altiore, longitudinem capitis æquante, pinna dorsali secunda usque ad pinnam dorsalem fere continuata.

Macrurus (Chalinura) simulus Goode et Bean.

(Oceanic Ichthyology‹ p. 412, fig. 345.)

Of this species the ‹Ingolf› expedition obtained 4 smaller specimens from

Stat. **18**: 61 44′Lat. N., 30 29′Long. W. (Entrance of Denmark Strait), 1135 fath., temp. at bottom 3 .o C. Further 2 specimens (280 og 160ᵐᵐ) from

Stat. **83**: 62˙25′Lat. N., 28 30′Long. W. (Denmark Strait), 912 fathoms, temp. at bottom 3 .5 C.
and 2 specimens (280 and 330ᵐᵐ) from

Stat. **91**: 64 44′ Lat. N., 31 Long. W. (Denmark Strait, 1236 fathoms, temp. at bottom 3 .1 C.

For the determination of this species I have made use of a specimen sent from the Museum at Washington. The head, whose length to the branchial cleft is contained almost 5 to fully 5 times in the total length, is thick with a rather long and obtusely rounded snout. The eyes are small, their diameter being only about a half frontal diameter. The mouth is very large and almost terminal, the snout being almost regularly truncate and only little protruding; the upper jaw wearing a card of teeth whose external teeth are exceedingly the largest, the lower jaw wearing a single row. The first dorsal numbers 11 rays, of which the first is very short and the second long and serrate as in most other Macrurids; the second dorsal begins at some distance from the first, the point of the first dorsal in its depressed state reaching to or a little beyond the beginning of the second. The first ray of the ventrals is produced in filiform shape and reaches not a little beyond the anus. The scales are rather small, but distinctly pluricarinate, specially in the head, which else shows some soft and naked parts: the preopercle, the margin of the jaws, parts of the snout and the whole lower surface of the head.

As to other localities the reader is referred to Oceanic Ichthyology p. 412.

Trachyrhynchus Murrayi Gthr.

(Deep-Sea Fishes, Challenger Report p. 153, pl. 41, fig. A.)

Of this species a young one (120ᵐᵐ) was obtained at station **73** (62 58′ Lat. N., 23 28′ Long. W., Southwest of Iceland at 486 fathoms, at a temperature at the bottom of 5 .5 C.). Previously it has been taken in the Faroe-Channel at a depth of 555 fathoms.

Gadoids and allied Fishes.

Motella (Onos) Reinhardti Kr. (Tab. IV, fig. 8).

Compare the description and figure in den norske Nordhavs Expedition , Fiskene, S. 131, pl. IV, fig. 34 and the Challenger Report p. 97, pl. XIX, fig. B.

After this Gadoid having been sent down from Greenland several times in earlier years, it was found again in the sea between Spitsbergen and Beeren-Island in the ice-cold water at a depth of 658 fathoms. Later it is found again in the Faroe-Channel at a depth of 540 640 fathoms. Ingolf obtained it in a few specimens on Station 116 (70°05′ Lat. North, 8 26′ Long. West, South of Jan Mayen, at 371 fathoms, brown Biloculina-mud, at a temperature at the bottom of ÷ 0°.4 C.) and at Station 140 (63 29′ Lat. North, 6 57′ Long. West, North of the Faroe Islands, 780 fathoms, gray mud and a bottom temperature of ÷ 0°.9 C.), also at Station 43 (West of the Faroe Islands, 61° 42′ Lat. North, 10 11′ Long. West, 645 fathoms, sandbottom (?), bottom temperature 0 .05 C.). Some young specimens were obtained at Station 2 (63 04′ Lat. North, 9° 22′ Long. W., 262 fathoms, Southeast of Iceland, clay and gravel, temperature at the bottom 5°.3 C.) and on Station 91 (Denmark Strait, 64°44′ Lat. N., 31 00′ Long. W., 1236 fathoms, Globigerina mud, bottom temperature 3°.1 C.). The new localities do not much extend the known geographical distribution, but seem to show, that it may occur at less considerable depths and under a less cold temperature, but also at somewhat greater depths and under low degrees of warmth, a little over or under zero. A sketch executed on the Ingolf gives it a light testaceous colour.

Of larves (on the so termed *Couchia*-stage) several were fished by the Ingolf of this or other arctic species, especially between the Faroe and the Shetland islands as well as east and south east of these and south of Iceland, at the surface. Of the other arctic *Motella*-species, *M. septentrionalis* Coll. and *M. cusis* Rhdt. (compare «Norske Nordhavs Expedition» p. 138, pl. IV, fig. 35—36; «Oceanic Ichthyology» p. 381, fig. 327) nothing new was ascertained through the Ingolf» Expeditions.

Haloporphyrus eques Gthr. (Tab. IV, fig. 7).

Of this species, known from the Report of the Challenger expedition (p. 91, pl. 18 B) the Ingolf expedition obtained on Station 9 (West of Iceland, Denmark Strait at 64 18′ Lat. North 27 00′ Long. W., at a depth of 295 fathoms, bottom clay, bottom temperature 5″.8 C.) two specimens $7^1/_4$ inch. long (one of them defect). Several larger and smaller specimens were obtained from the stations 81 and **89**, at 61 44′ Lat. North, 27°00′ Long. West, 485 fathoms, bottom temperature 6′.1 C. and 64° 45′ Lat. North, 27 20′ Long. West, 310 fathoms, bottom temperature 8 .4 C., partly from Denmark Strait, West of Iceland, partly southwest of this island. Previously the species is taken (specimens 12—13 inches long) in the Faroe-Channel at a depth of 530 fathoms and later in Gascony bay at depths of 1410 and 800 metres (Koehler, Résultats scientifiques de la Campagne du Caudan fasc. III, 1896). Nearly related types are known from the Mediterranean: *H. lepidion* Risso (cfr. Vinciguerra: Anal. Mus. Civico Genova vol. XVIII, p. 554, pl. III) and *H. Güntheri* Gigl. (can obtain a length of 24 inches, Günther, Report p. 91, pl. 18, fig. B; also off Portugal and at Madera). From more distant localities are known *H. cuosiuæ* Gthr. (Günther, l. c. pl. XX, fig. B, 12 inches, Inosima, 345 fathoms) and *H. ensiferus* Gthr. (l. c. pl. XIX, fig. A, mouth of Plata River, 600 fathoms).

Of one of the largest Ingolfian specimen I shall insert some measures.

Total length 275ᵐᵐ, head 63ᵐᵐ, consequently not $^1/_4$ of the total length.

Diameter of the eye 21ᵐᵐ, $^1/_3$ of the length of the head, a little more than the length of the snout (20ᵐᵐ) and about $1^1/_2$ time the interorbital space.

The upper jaw terminating below the anterior margin of the lens; the filamentous ray of the ventrals c. 35ᵐᵐ, the pectoral 44ᵐᵐ (about equal to the length of the head without the snout); the length of the first dorsal ray equals the length of the head.

A sketch made on the expedition gives to the fish a chocolate-brown colour with a bluish tint especially on the fins.

Antimora viola Goode & Bean.

The genus *Antimora* numbers two species, a southern and a northern, if really different, a question, on which Dr. Günther apparently speaks with some diffidence. They really must be very nearly related, but I have no doubt that the Ingolfian specimens are here correctly determined. *A. rostrata* Günther (Report on deep-sea fishes p. 93, pl. XVI A) was found off the mouth of the Plata River and off Montevideo, at a depth of 600 fathoms, between Kerguelen and Cape, and in the neighbourhood of Marion Island at 1375 fathoms; the largest specimen was 24 Engl. inches. *A. viola* G. & B. (ibid. p. 94, pl. 15) was first captured at a depth of 4—500 fathoms on the edge of ele Havre bank , later in 25 specimens in localities between 33 35′ Lat. North and 41°34′ Lat. North and between 76° 00′ Long. West and 65° 54′ Long. West at depths between 306 and 1242 fathoms. The expedition of the prince of Monaco (Collett, Résultats des campagnes scientifiques etc. p. 59) obtained 12 specimens a little more to the north (45° 20′ Lat. North) on the Newfoundland bank at a depth of 1267 meters; the largest specimen was 358ᵐᵐ.

The stations from which Ingolf has brought home Antimores, 6 specimens in all, are

Station	Lat. N.	Long. W.		Fathoms		Temp. of bottom
50:	62° 43′	15° 07′	(South of Iceland)	1020	Gray mud with basalt grains	3°.13 C.
76:	60° 50′	26° 50′	(Southwest of Iceland)	806	Gray mud	4°.1 C.
83:	62° 25′	28° 30′	(Likewise)	912	Gray mud	3°.5 C.
93:	64° 24′	35° 14′	(Denmark Strait)	767	Gray mud	1°.46 C.

All these localities are, as it will be seen, south, southwest or west of Iceland though one of them rather near to the coast of East-Greenland. The largest specimen has a length of 15¹/₂ inch. When the first dorsal ray is well preserved it proves to be considerably larger than it is figured in *Antimora viola* (comp. the figure of *Haloporphyrus viola* in Goodes «The fisheries and fishery industries of the United States», Sect. I, pl. 64).

Rhodichthys regina Coll. (Tab. III, fig. 4).

Of this species, which is classed with the *Brotulidæ*, and which was discovered by the Norwegian North sea expedition in the sea between Beeren Island and Finmarken at a depth of 1280 fathoms (Biloculina-clay, bottom temperature ÷ 1°.4), only this single specimen (297ᵐᵐ) was known which is described and figured by Prof. Collett (den norske Nordhavs Expedition , Fiskene, p. 154, pl. V, fig. 37—39). The Ingolf expedition brought home several more or less well preserved specimens; the length of the largest does not exceed 122ᵐᵐ. In one of them the left ventral is tripartite instead of bipartite, as usual. They are not uniformly red as the original type of the species, but spotted or figured, with small brownish spots, which interrupt the reddish bottom colour of the skin. The number of vertebræ of the body is between 9 and 11, of the tail between 53 and 58. The localities are the following:

Station	Lat. N.	Long. W.		Fathoms	Condition of the bottom	Temp. of the bottom.
104:	66° 23′	7° 25′	(East of Iceland)	957	Light grayish brown mud	÷ 1°.1 C.
105:	65° 34′	7° 31′	(Likewise)	762	Light brown mud	÷ 0°.8 C.
111:	67° 14′	8° 48′	(Likewise)	860	Brown Biloculina-clay	÷ 0°.9 C.
117:	69° 13′	8° 23′	(South of Jan Mayen)	1003	Light Biloculina-clay	÷ 1°.0 C.
118:	68° 27′	8° 20′	(Between Iceland and Jan Mayen)	1060	Light Biloculina-clay	÷ 1°.0 C.
119:	67° 53′	10° 19′	(Likewise)	1010	Light Biloculina-clay	÷ 1°.0 C.
120:	67° 29′	11° 32′	(Likewise)	885	Light Biloculina-clay	÷ 1°.0 C.
140:	63° 29′	6° 57′	(North of Faroe Island)	780	Gray mud	÷ 0°.9 C.

Colloïdei (s. l.).

Sebastes marinus L. (norvegicus Ascan.)

was found at the following places, Davis Strait, off Holsteinsborg, by the Ingolf expedition :

Station	Lat. N.	Long. W.	fathoms		temp. at bottom
31:	66 35′	55 54′	88		1 .6 C.
32:	66 35′	56 38′	318	Brown gray mud with *Rhabdammina*	3°.9 C.
34:	67 17′	54 17′	55		0°.9 C.

The arctic-ichthyological literature often cited will illustrate sufficiently the geographical and bathymetric distribution of the redfish. It is known besides from Greenland, from Iceland, from Spitsbergen and Beeren Island, from the whole Norwegian coast, from the Danish shores (occasionally), from the Irish and North-british coasts and· from the eastern coast of North America to Cape Cod (cfr. the enumeration of the stations in »Oceanic Ichthyology« p. 261) in so far that it is not the *S. vi-viparus*, which here represents the type. I shall not here repeat what I have formerly said (Vidensk. Medd. Naturh. Foren. , 1876) of the difference between the true redfish and Lysougeren (*S. viviparus*) - may this be a distinct species or a fjord or shore variety of *S. marinus* but only remark, that *S. viviparus* is found at the Faroe Islands, at the coast of Norway and Bohuslän and at the coast of New England (specimens from Eastport and Gloucester sent me from the Smithsonian Institution), but so far known not at the coast of Finmarken or of Great Britain. Small ones of *S. marinus* were taken in the nets south and southwest of Iceland and in the open sea at Denmark Strait.

Phobetor ventralis C. V. (tricuspis Rhdt.).

This arctic sea-scorpion has not been brought home with the ‹Ingolf›, but it may nevertheless reasonably be mentioned here. My remarks on its relation to *Cottus pistilliger* Pall. (Videnskab. Meddelelser 1876) have occasioned that it is named *Gymnacanthus pistilliger* (Collett: »Norske Nordhavs-Expedition , Fiskene, p. 26, and elsewhere). As I have said that there was no experience of its being fished at a greater depth than 20 fathoms, I will add that we have obtained young ones of this species in Baffin Strait at 50 fathoms, and that »den norske Nordhavs-Expedition« has obtained it at the same depth at Spitsbergen. On Ryder's expedition to East-Greenland a specimen was taken at the shore of Hold with Hope on very low water. For its other known geographical distribution my remarks in Videnskab. Naturh. Foren. 1876, p. 365 may be consulted, also Collett l. c. p. 28. Also the works of Lilljeborg and Smitt may naturally be consulted for facts of this nature. It is thus known from different East- and West-Greenland-localities and from places in Arctic America, at Labrador and Nova Scotia, in the Fundy Bay, at Iceland, Finmarken, Novaja Semlia, in the Behring Sea, at Kamschatka and — if no mistake — at Japan. In Gilbert's ›The ichthyological collections of the U. S. Fish. C. S. ›Albatross , Report of the U. S. Commission of fish and fisheries for 1893 an other species is mentioned from Unalaska, *Gymnacanthus galeatus* Bean, which is said to be nearer related to *P. tricuspis* than to *P. pistilliger* . It is stated, it must be observed, by this author in agreement with Dresel (Proceed. Un. St. Nat. Museum 1884, p. 250), that the North-atlantic type (*G. tricuspis*) differs specifically from the Northpacific (*G. pistilliger*). I refer the reader to the notes of Gilbert (l. c. p. 424). As I have also previously bespoken the relation between *Phobetor (Gymnacanthus)* and the species *Cottus claviger* and *C. diceræus*, I shall further add, that these two species now (Gilbert l. c. p. 426) are cited as species of a genus *Enophrys*.

Cottunculus microps Coll.

Cottus or *Cottunculus microps* is first (1875) established (Collett: Norges Fiske, med Bemærkninger om deres Udbredelse, Tillæg til Videnskab. Selsk. Forhandl. 1874, p. 20, pl. 1, fig. 3) on a very young sea-scorpion, fished by Mr. O. Sars at the depth of 200 fathoms in the vicinity of Hammersfest. Afterwards den norske Nordhavs-Expedition (l. c. p. 18—25, pl. 1, fig. 5—6) obtained it in 3 specimens, taken Northwest of Hammersfest and West of Norskoen (Spitsbergen) at depths from 191 to 459 fathoms (size 93—175^{mm}); the bottom sandy or grayish blue clay, the temperature at the bottom ÷ 0.1 à 3°.5 C. Still later it was found in the Faroe-Channel, so called, by an English expedition (Günther: Report, Challenger, p. 60, t. IX, fig. A) and by an American expedition still nearer to the American side, two small specimens from a depth of 260 fathoms, 39° 59' Lat. N. and 70° 18' Long. W. (Tarleton Bean and Brown Goode: Report on the results of dredging, Bull. Mus. Compar. Zool. 1883, p. 212). From Greenland itself we have obtained 3 specimens (200—260^{mm}) sent down by M. Müller, inspector of the colony Sukkertoppen, and Prof. F. Smitt states (Skandinaviens Fiskar I, p. 159), that a male of the length of 157^{mm} was taken on Nordenskiöld's expedition on the eastcoast of Greenland at 130 fathoms depth on clay bottom and at 65° 30' Long. North. The most northern point where this sea-scorpion of the cold and deep sea is known is 80° Lat. North (Spitsbergen), the most southern on the European side is the Trondhjemsfjord (63½°); according to the statement of F. Smitt it is there taken in rather numerous specimens at depths from 100—200 fathoms. After a note by T. Bean (Notice of the remarkable marine fauna occupying the outer banks of the southern coast of New England, Nr. 2; American Journal of Science, October 1881, p. 296) it is taken at 7 stations at the depth of 310—396 fathoms on the banks off the southcoast of New England. Günther (l. c.) also states, that several specimens are known from the southcoast of New England at depths from 238 to 372 fathoms. Compare also Oceanic Ichthyology, p. 269, fig. 257 and 261 a, b.

This species is figured by Collett at the places cited in Norges Fiske and in den norske Nordhavs Expedition, by Günther in the deep-sea fishes of the Challenger (l. c.), and by F. Smitt (Skandinaviens Fiskar, I, p. 158, fig. 45), further in Oceanic Ichthyology pl. 1. As it is also described by the said authors, by Lilljeborg and by Jordan and Gilbert (Synopsis of the fishes of North America 1882, p. 688) I may limit myself to an enumeration of the Ingolfian localities and to the addition of a few descriptive notes.

The skin is densely rough everywhere on the head, body and tail, weakest on the belly, from small round asperities; at some places they are grouped together in small heaps and may be continued on the dorsal rays — more sparsely on the pectorals. The interorbital space is rather large. Behind the eyes is found an arc of 4 coniform knobs; somewhat more behind, on the occiput, are two and at both sides in a line with the upper end of the branchial cleft one or two smaller knobs with some more

farther down at the inferior part of the preopercle. In the young ones they are hardly to be distinguished with the exception of two tubercles behind the eyes. There are four dark-coloured bands,
one over the base of the tail, one over the hind part of the dorsal fin and downwards to the anal
fin, a third over the foremost part of the dorsal down towards the pectorals and a fourth — especially
distinct in the younger   transversely over the front, the eyes and the cheeks.

The Stations of *C. microps* at the Ingolf voyages were:

Stat. Lat. N. Long. W.

9: 64 18′ 27 00′ (West of Iceland), 295 fathoms, clay, bottom temp. 5˚.8 C. (size 45 and 30^{mm}).

28: 65 14′ 55 12′ (West of Sukkertoppen), 420 fathoms, soft brown gray mud with many *Rhabdam-
minæ*, bottom temp. 3 .5 C. (45^{mm}).

32: 66 35′ 56 38′ (Davis Strait, off Holsteinsborg), 318 fathoms, brown gray mud with many *Rhabdam-
minæ*, bottom temp. 3 .9 C., male and female (160 and 80^{mm}).

35: 65 16′ 55 05′ (Southwest of Sukkertoppen), 362 fath., brownish mud with arenaceous foraminifera,
bottom temp. 3 .6 C. (52^{mm}).

126: 67 19′ 15 52′ (North of Iceland), 293 fathoms, gray brown, blue claylike mud, bottom temperature
+ 0˚.5 C., female (154^{mm}).

141: 63 22′ 6 58′ (North of the Faroe Islands), 679 fath., gray mud, bottom tp. + 0˚.6 C., male (170^{mm}).

Cottunculus torvus Goode (Thompsoni Günther)

was described almost contemporaneously under the name cited, by Brown Goode and Tarleton
Bean (Report on the results of dredging under the supervision of Alex. Agassiz, Report on the fishes,
Bulletin of the Museum of Comparative Zoology , X, 5, 1883, p. 213) and by Alb. Günther (Report
on the deep-sea fishes, the voyage of H. M. S. ·Challenger , 1887, p. 61, pl. XI, fig. B). It is figured by
Günther and by Léon Vaillant (Expéditions scientifiques du Travailleur et du Talisman 1880—83,
Poissons (1888), p. 361, pl. 28, fig. 3), whose figure however, as stated in the text, is defective, the artist
having overlooked the first part of the dorsal. The localities, from which this species is known, are
1) The ·Faroe Channel· at 535 fathoms depth (size 7¹⁄₂ inches). 2) The 5 specimens of the length of
62—407^{mm}, fished by the American deep-sea expeditions at 464 ·723 fathoms at 33˚ 42′ Lat. North to
41 32′ Lat. North and at 65 55′ Long. West to 76˚ Long. W. 3) The French expeditions obtained 9
specimens (35—146^{mm}) off the Sudan coast and at the ·banc d'Arguin at depths of 1139—1459 metres.
4) With the Fylla· a specimen, 150^{mm} lang, was obtained in Davis Strait (66˚ 49′ Lat. North, 56˚ 28′
Long. West, at a depth of 235 fathoms, sand and ooze bottom, bottom temp. 4 .4 C.) (Vidensk. Meddel.
fra den naturh. Forening· 1891, p. 29). 5) With Ingolf· finally a specimen was obtained, a female,
184^{mm}, at station **83** (Denmark Strait, South west of Iceland), 62 25′ Lat. North, 28˚ 30′ Long. West,
depth 912 fathoms, temperature at the bottom 3 .5 C.

This *Cottunculus* is smooth without granulations etc., light gray without designs; the head is
strongly provided with coniform tubercles on front, top and sides of the head, opercles etc. A specimen
from the American deep-sea expeditions has been before me for comparison; young specimens are
not at hand.

Cottunculus inermis Vaill.

was hitherto only known from the description and figure of Vaillant (l. c. p. 365, pl. 28, fig. 2) and was misjudged by the authors of «Oceanic Ichthyology» (p. 525) who identified it with *C. microps*. The French expeditions obtained 3 specimens (86^{mm} in length) from the localities already cited (the coast of Sudan and «Banc d'Arguin») at a depth of 930 and 1.195 metres. More northerly it was hitherto unknown. Ingolf» obtained 4 specimens:

Stat. Lat. N. Long. W.

102: 66 23′ 10 26′ (East of Cape Langanæs), 750 fath., brown mud, bottom temp. + 0 .9 C., size 58^{mm}.

104: 66 23′ 7 25′ (East of the northeastpoint of Iceland), 957 fathoms, light graybrown mud, bottom temperature ÷ 1 .1 C., female, size 94^{mm}.

125: 68 08′ 16° 02′ (North of Iceland), 729 fathoms, bottom brown mud, temp. ÷ 0°.8 C., a female, 150^{mm}, and a younger specimen, 50^{mm}.

Uniformly grayish without any design, almost quite naked and smooth, only a very little rough to the sense of feeling. No tubercles either on the crown of the head, the occiput or opercles. The distance between the small eyes is very large, more than thrice a diameter of the eye. Palatal teeth not observed. Could therefore on so termed technical reasons be cut off as a peculiar generic type, but I prefer with Vaillant to keep it in the genus *Cottunculus*. It may still be added that in younger specimens the granulation is very distinct and dense, though not so dense and complete as in *C. microps*.

A note about the northern Cotti.

Cottus scorpius L. That the Greenland sea-scorpion (*C. grønlandicus*) is not specifically different from the common North-european species is well known now-a-days, though it may still happen that now and then a „Cottus grønlandicus" is mentioned from European (Norwegian, Scottish, English) localities, most likely in cases where uncommon large specimens of *C. scorpius* have occurred. The „Ingolf" expedition has brought home specimens of this species from stat. **33** (67 57′ Lat. North, 55 30′ Long. West, S. W. of Egedesminde, depth 35 fathoms, gray sand bottom, bottom temperature o°.8 C.). From the east coast of Greenland (Jameson's Land, „Hekla's harbour" etc., from the shore to the depth of some [11] fathoms) the expedition of Ryder brought home some specimens, partly young ones, partly rather adult individuals. It is added, that in „Hekla's harbour" it was found the whole year round. *C. scorpius* is otherwise known from almost the whole west coast of Greenland to Umanak and Upernivik, it is noted from Boothia, Port Leopold, the Wellington channel and the Northumberland sound, on the eastern side of America to Cape Hatteras, at Iceland. Spitsbergen, the White Sea and Novaja-Semlia, at the Faroe-Islands and at the British coasts to the mouth of the „Channel" and at the Scandinavian shores, in the Baltic to Uleåborg. If the „Jaok" of the Kamtschadales (*C. jaoc*) is correctly referred by Malmgrén to our common sea-scorpion, it meets in the northern part of the Pacific with several other species of *Cottus*, for which I must refer to the literature, as it would be too prolix to make a detailed account of it at this place.

C. scorpioides Fabr. (on which I must refer to my elucidations in „Vidensk. Meddel. Naturh. Forening" 1876) was not found by the „Ingolf" expedition, nor are there from other sources turned up any new informations on it. That Dr. F. Smitt (l. c.) regards it as a variety of *C. scorpius* does, after what I have set forth formerly, of course not agree with my conception.

C. Lilljeborgii has not been found on any of our arctic expeditions. On the other hand it is named (Proc. Royal Soc. Edinburgh, Vol. XV, p. 207, tab. IV, fig. B) between the deep-sea fishes obtained on the north coast of Scottland by Murray.

Cottus quadricornis L. has not been found neither by the „Ingolf" expedition. On the other hand the expedition of Ryder to East-Greenland obtained a specimen at the depth of 3—6 fathoms at „Hekla's harbour" („Meddelelser om Gronland", XIX, Hvirveldyr by E. Bay p. 52). Otherwise it is well known that it has been found at

Melville island and near the „Copper mine" (67 12' Lat. North) in the Gulf of Bothnia and in the adjoining part of the Baltic, in the Swedish and Russian lakes, in the White Sea and at Novaja-Semlia. Cfr. my former communication the on the northern Cottoids in „Vidensk. Meddel. Naturh. Forening" 1876. Further information on its distribution at the east coast of Greenland may probably be awaited through a future Eastgreenland expedition.

Icelus hamatus Kr.

The places where this little arctic *Cottoid* was obtained at the Ingolf expedition were:

Station	Lat. N.	Long. W.		fathoms		bottom temp.
31:	66° 35'	55° 54'	off Holsteinsborg	88		1 .6 C.
33:	67 57'	55° 30'	S.W. of Egedesminde	35	gray sand	o .8 C.
34:	67° 17'	54 17'	off Holsteinsborg	55		o .8 C.
127:	66° 33'	20° 05'	North of Iceland	44	sand bottom	5°.6 C.

Other informations on its distribution and occurrence will be found in the report of the Dijmphna expedition and in the Norwegian North-Sea expedition, in Oceanic Ichthyology etc. In the last cited work and in Gilbert's report on the fish-collections made in the northern part of the Pacific (at Alaska, Unalaska etc.) it is named *Icelus bicornis* (Reinhardt), the author probably following the hypothetical suggestion by Collett, that an *Icelus* may have been the foundation of Reinhardt's *Cottus bicornis*, which can not be determined with certainty, the original specimen not existing. To change a denomination of scientific certitude with another of dubious applicability can only involve uncertainty and want of clearness. Gilbert also infers the possibility that the Pacific type might differ specifically from the Atlantic North-Sea type. There are further named by North-american ichthyologists quite a series of Northpacific species: *Icelus spiniger, canaliculatus, vicinalis, euryops* and *scutiger, Icelinus borealis, tenuis, filamentosus, fimbriatus* and *oculatus*, as well as some species of new genera unknown to me. The relation between those representative species from the same region of both oceans is, it is true, of great interest, but requires for its solution a relatively great material placed in one single hand.

Artediellus (Centridermichthys) uncinatus (Rhdt.). (Tab. IV, fig. 9.)

Of this small Cottoid many specimens were captured at station 33 (67 57' Lat. North, 55° 30' Long. West, at a depth of 35 fathoms, on gray sand, at a temperature at the bottom of o .8 C.), some at station 29 (65 34' Lat. North, 54 31' Long. West, depth 68 fathoms, on sandy bottom, temperature at the bottom o .2 C.) and a single specimen at station 31 (66° 35' Lat. North, 55° 54' Long. West, at 88 fathoms, temperature of bottom 1 .6 C.), all on localities off the west coast of Greenland, not farther south than Sukkertoppen, not farther north than Egedesminde. On its occurrence elsewhere may be referred to my former Meddelelser om nordiske Ulkefiske (Vidensk. Medd. Naturh. Forening 1876, Novaja Semlia, coast of Norway down to 59) and to Bidrag til Kundskab om Kara Havets Fiske (Dijmphna-Togtet 1886, p. 124, west coast of Novaja Semlia); to Collett: (den norske Nordhavs-Expedition , Fiskene, p. 29, between North Cape and Spitsbergen) and his Meddelelser om Norges Fiske (Nyt Magasin for Naturvidensk. Bd. 29, 1884); also Hubrecht (Niederl. Archiv f. Zoologie,

Suppl. Bd., 1882, east of Beeren Island) and Bay (l. c., East Greenland, 127 fathoms, 74 ̊ 17' Lat. North, 15 ̊ 20' Long. West). In Oceanic Ichthyology (p. 267) numerous localities from various northatlantic places are cited. As a synonym *Cottus bicornis* Rhdt. is also cited here; concerning this the reader is referred to what is remarked above on *Icelus hamatus*.

Triglops Pingelii (Rhdt).

was found by Ingolf> at the following localities:

Stat.	Lat. N.	Long. W.		fathoms	Bottom	bottom temp.	
29:	65 ̊ 34'	54 ̊ 31'	off Sukkertoppen	68	sand	0 .2 C.	1 specimen.
33:	67 ̊ 57'	55 30'	S.W. of Egedesminde	35	gray sand	0 .8 C.	Numerous specimens of both sexes and younger stages.
34:	67 ̊ 17'	54 ̊ 17'	off Holsteinsborg	55	sandy	0 .9 C.	8 specimens.

From the earlier literature it will be seen, that *Triglops Pingelii* is found not only on the west coast of Greenland, but also from Spitsbergen, from the Barents Sea (East and South of Beeren Island), from the sea East and South of Jan Mayen, at Iceland, northern Norway to Christianssund at South, at the Faroe Islands, and at the Northamerican shores. A long list of Eastamerican localities are cited from the western Atlantic to the latitude of New England. A *Tr. pleurosticus* Cope from Godhavn has been put on record (Proc. Acad. Philad. 1865), but in Oceanic Ichthyology (p. 269) it is as by myself (Vidensk. Medd. Naturhist. Forening 1876, p. 378) withdrawn to *Tr. Pingelii*. A new species (*Tr. Murrayi* Gthr.) has meanwhile been established (Report of fishes obtained in deep water on the Northwest coast of Scotland, Proc. Roy. Soc. Edinburgh XV, p. 209, tab. IV, fig. A) on a form found in Mull of Cantyre at 64 fathoms and Southeast of the island of Souda, said to be distinguished by a lesser number of rays, the size of the eyes, another shape of the head and a more compressed tail. From the northern part of the Pacific is cited *Tr. Beani* (Gilbert: Ichthyological collections p. 426, t. 28), *Tr. scepticus* (p. 428, pl. 28) and *Tr. xenostethus* (p. 429, pl. 29); the 2 first named of these species at least are established on a greater number of specimens.

Agonus decagonus Bl.

is fished on the following places:

Station	Lat. N.	Long. W.		fathoms		bottom temp.	
31:	66 ̊ 35'	55 ̊ 54'	Davis Strait	88		1 ̊.6 C.	
125:	66 08'	16 02'	North of Iceland	729	brown mud	÷ 0 .8 C.	
126:	67 ̊ 19'	15 52'	Likewise	293	graybrown mud	÷ 0 ̊.5 C.	
143:	62 58'	7 09'	North of Faroe islands	388	sandy botom	÷ 0 .4 C.	Two younger specimens.

In Oceanic Ichthyology placed in the genus *Podothecus*. Outside of Greenland known from Spitsbergen, the Barents Sea, Iceland, Varangerfjord and West-Finmarken. *A. malarmoides* Deslongchamps, probably the same species, is said to be from Newfoundland (cfr. Vidensk. Meddel. 1876, p. 381). On other mailed Cottoids in the northern part of the Pacific the cited works of Gilbert, Jordan and Starks may be consulted.

Aspidophoroides monopterygius Lac.

Beyond the sea of the west coast of Greenland, where it is collected several times (Vidensk. Meddel. l. c. p. 385) and where the Ingolf expedition has obtained it at station 31 (Davis Strait, 66 35′ Lat. North, 55 54′ Long. West, South of Egedesminde, at a depth of 88 fathoms and a bottom temperature of 1.6 C.) and at station 33 (67 57′ Lat. North, 55 30′ Long. West, on 35 fathoms, South-west of Egedesminde, on gray sand, at a bottom temperature of o.8 C., it is found repeatedly in the sea of the eastern coast of Northamerica, even South of Cape Cod (Oceanic Ichthyology p. 284). From Vancouvers Island is known a *A. (Angelogonus) inermis* and from the west coast of America further *A. Güntheri* Bean.

Aspidophoroides Olrikii Ltk.

known from the Greenland sea (Hellefiskebankerne, 32 fathoms depth) (Vidensk. Meddel. Naturhist. Foren. 1876, p. 386). the Kara Sea (Dijmphna , Kara Havets Fiske- p. 120, pl. XV, Fig. 1—3) and the Barents Sea. Was captured plentifully at stat. 33 (cfr. above). A dubious specimen is mentioned in Oceanic Ichthyology (p. 284) from a depth of 44 fathoms at 46 45′ Lat. North and 50 02′ 30″ Long. West. The prince of Monaco obtained 2 specimens on the banks of Newfoundland (Collett, Résultats des Camp. scientif. p. 39). It is cited also from the White Sea and the eastern part of the Murmannian sea (Verzeichniss der Fische des weissen und murmanschen Meeres; l'Annuaire du Musée zoologique de St. Pétersbourg 1897).

Aspidophoroides Olrikii.

Contents.

The Ichthyological Results of the Expeditions of the ,,Ingolf".

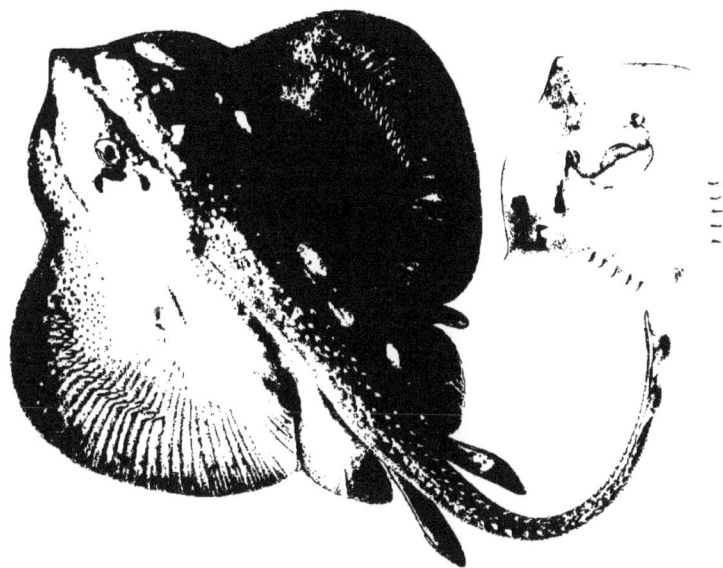

THE INGOLF-EXPEDITION

1895—1896.

THE LOCALITIES, DEPTHS, AND BOTTOMTEMPERATURES OF THE STATIONS.

Station Nr.	Lat. N.	Long. W.	Depth in Danish fathoms	Bottom-temp.	Station Nr.	Lat. N.	Long. W.	Depth in Danish fathoms	Bottom-temp.	Station Nr.	Lat. N.	Long. W.	Depth in Danish fathoms	Bottom-temp.
1	62° 30'	8° 21'	132	7°2	24	63° 06'	56° 00'	1199	2°4	45	61° 32'	9° 43'	643	4°17
2	63° 04'	9° 22'	262	5°3	25	63° 30'	54° 25'	582	3°3	46	61° 32'	11° 36'	720	2°40
3	63° 35'	10° 24'	272	0°5		63° 51'	53° 03'	136		47	61° 32'	13° 40'	950	3°23
4	64° 07'	11° 12'	237	2°5	26	63° 57'	52° 41'	34	0°6	48	61° 32'	15° 11'	1150	3°17
5	64° 40'	12° 09'	155			64° 37'	54° 24'	109		49	62° 07'	15° 07'	1120	2°91
6	63° 43'	14° 34'	90	7°0	27	64° 54'	55° 10'	393	3°8	50	62° 43'	15° 07'	1020	3°13
7	63° 13'	15° 41'	600	4°5	28	65° 14'	55° 42'	420	305	51	64° 15'	14° 22'	68	7°32
8	63° 56'	24° 40'	136	6°0	29	65° 34'	54° 31'	68	0°2	52	63° 57'	13° 32'	420	7°87
9	64° 18'	27° 00'	295	5°8	30	66° 50'	54° 28'	22	1°05	53	63° 15'	15° 07'	795	3°08
10	64° 24'	28° 50'	788	3°5	31	66° 35'	55° 54'	88	1°6	54	63° 08'	15° 40'	691	3°9
11	64° 34'	31° 12'	1300	1°6	32	66° 35'	56° 38'	318	3°9	55	63° 33'	15° 02'	316	5°9
12	64° 38'	32° 37'	1040	0°3	33	67° 57'	55° 30'	35	0°8	56	64° 00'	15° 09'	68	7°57
13	64° 47'	34° 33'	622	3°0	34	65° 17'	54° 17'	55		57	63° 37'	13° 02'	350	3°4
14	64° 45'	35° 05'	176	4°4	35	65° 16'	55° 05'	362	3°6	58	64° 25'	12° 09'	211	0°8
15	66° 18'	25° 59'	330	-0°75	36	61° 50'	56° 21'	1435	1°5	59	65° 00'	11° 16'	310	-0°1
16	65° 43'	26° 58'	250	6°1	37	60° 17'	54° 05'	1715	1°4	60	65° 09'	12° 27'	124	0°9
17	62° 49'	26° 55'	745	3°4	38	59° 12'	51° 05'	1870	1°3	61	65° 03'	13° 06'	55	0°4
18	61° 44'	30° 29'	1135	3°0	39	62° 00'	22° 38'	865	2°9	62	63° 18'	19° 12'	72	7°92
19	60° 29'	34° 14'	1566	2°4	40	62° 00'	21° 36'	845	3°3	63	62° 40'	19° 05'	800	4°0
20	58° 20'	40° 48'	1695	1°5	41	61° 39'	17° 10'	1245	2°0	64	62° 06'	19° 00'	1041	3°1
21	58° 01'	44° 45'	1330	2°4	42	61° 41'	10° 17'	625	0°4	65	61° 33'	19° 00'	1689	3°0
22	58° 10'	48° 25'	1845	1°4	43	61° 42'	10° 11'	645	0°05	66	61° 33'	20° 43'	1128	3°3
23	60° 43'	56° 00'	Only the Plankton Net used		44	61° 42'	9° 36'	545	4°8	67	61° 30'	22° 30'	975	3°0

Station Nr.	Long. W.	Lat. N.	Depth in Danish fathoms	Bottom-temp.	Station Nr.	Lat. N.	Long. W.	Depth in Danish fathoms	Bottom-temp.	Station Nr.	Lat. N.	Long. W.	Depth in Danish fathoms	Bottom-temp.
68	62° 06'	22° 30'	843	3°4	92	64° 44'	32° 52'	976	1°4	118	68° 27'	8° 20'	1060	-1°0
69	62° 40'	22° 17'	589	3°9	93	64° 24'	35° 14'	767	1°46	119	67° 53'	10° 19'	1010	-1°0
70	63° 09'	22° 05'	134	7°0	94	64° 56'	36° 19'	204	4°1	120	67° 29'	11° 32'	885	-1°0
71	63° 46'	22° 03'	46			65° 31'	30° 45'	213		121	66° 59'	13° 11'	529	-0°7
72	63° 12'	23° 04'	197	6°7	95	65° 14'	30° 39'	752	2°1	122	66° 42'	14° 44'	115	1°8
73	62° 58'	23° 28'	486	5°5	96	65° 24'	29° 00'	735	1°2	123	66° 52'	15° 40'	145	2°0
74	62° 17'	24° 36'	695	4°2	97	65° 28'	27° 39'	450	5°5	124	67° 40'	15° 40'	495	-0°6
	61° 57'	25° 35'	761		98	65° 38'	26° 27'	138	5°9	125	68° 08'	16° 02'	729	-0°8
	61° 28'	25° 06'	829		99	66° 13'	25° 53'	187	6°1	126	67° 19'	15° 52'	293	-0°5
75	61° 28'	26° 25'	780	4°3	100	66° 23'	14° 02'	59	0°4	127	66° 33'	20° 05'	44	5°6
76	60° 50'	26° 50'	806	4°1	101	66° 23'	12° 05'	537	-0°7	128	66° 50'	20° 02'	194	0°6
77	60° 10'	26° 59'	951	3°6	102	66° 23'	10° 26'	750	-0°9	129	66° 35'	23° 47'	117	6°5
78	60° 37'	27° 52'	799	4°5	103	66° 23'	8° 52'	579	-0°6	130	63° 01'	20° 40'	338	6°55
79	60° 52'	28° 58'	653	4°4	104	66° 23'	7° 25'	957	-1°1	131	63° 00'	19° 09'	698	4°7
80	61° 02'	29° 32'	935	4°0	105	65° 34'	7° 31'	762	-0°8	132	63° 00'	17° 04'	747	4°6
81	61° 44'	27° 00'	485	6°1	106	65° 34'	8° 54'	447	-0°6	133	63° 14'	11° 24'	230	2°2
82	61° 55'	27° 28'	824	4°1		65° 29'	8° 40'	466		134	62° 34'	10° 26'	299	4°1
83	62° 25'	28° 30'	912	3°5	107	65° 33'	10° 28'	492	-0°3	135	62° 48'	9° 48'	270	0°4
	62° 36'	26° 01'	472		108	65° 30'	12° 00'	97	1°1	136	63° 01'	9° 11'	256	4°8
	62° 36'	25° 30'	401		109	65° 29'	13° 25'	38	1°5	137	63° 14'	8° 31'	297	-0°6
84	62° 58'	25° 24'	633	4°8	110	66° 44'	11° 33'	781	-0°8	138	63° 26'	7° 56'	471	-0°6
85	63° 21'	25° 21'	170		111	67° 14'	8° 48'	860	-0°9	139	63° 36'	7° 30'	702	-0°6
86	65° 03'6	23° 47'6	76		112	67° 57'	6° 44'	1267	-1°1	140	63° 29'	6° 57'	780	-0°9
87	65° 02'3	23° 56'2	110		113	69° 31'	7° 06'	1309	-1°0	141	63° 22'	6° 58'	679	-0°6
88	64° 58'	24° 25'	76	6°9	114	70° 36'	7° 29'	773	-1°0	142	63° 07'	7° 05'	587	-0°6
89	64° 45'	27° 20'	310	8°4	115	70° 50'	8° 29'	86	0°1	143	62° 58'	7° 09'	388	-0°4
90	64° 45'	29° 06'	568	4°4	116	70° 05'	8° 26'	371	-0°4	144	62° 49'	7° 12'	276	1°6
91	64° 44'	31° 00'	1236	3°1	117	69° 13'	8° 23'	1003	-1°0					

— ➤○◆○◀ — —

www.ingramcontent.com/pod-product-compliance
Lightning Source LLC
Chambersburg PA
CBHW031817090426
42739CB00008B/1309